Colin Wintle   Drawings by Nicola Luscombe

Around Historic Somerset and Avon

BELL & HYMAN · London

Illustrator

Nicola Luscombe was born in 1959 and lives in Tunbridge Wells. At present she is following a course in fine art at Canterbury Art College with a view to obtaining a Degree in Art.

She would like to become an illustrator of children's books.

In the same illustrated series

Around Historic Sussex, Ray Miller and Gerald Lip
Around Historic Hampshire, Colin Wintle and Victor Spink
Around Historic Lancashire, David Jessop
Around Historic Yorkshire, Jeffrey Lee and Leslie Coldrick
Around Historic Devon and Cornwall, Desmond Post and Stuart Richmond
Around Historic Kent, Malcolm John and C. A. T. Brigden
Around the Historic Chilterns, Ron Pigram

Front Cover illustration: Widcombe Manor
Title page illustration: Medieval Dovecot, Dunster

m

First published 1978 by
MIDAS BOOKS
12 Dene Way, Speldhurst
Tunbridge Wells, Kent TN3 0NX

ISBN 0 85936 088 1

Designed and produced by Mechanick Exercises London

Printed in Great Britain by Tonbridge Printers Limited, Peach Hall Works Tonbridge Kent

INTRODUCTION

April the First – All Fools' Day – in 1974 marked the abolition or emasculation of some ancient counties and the creation of new ones up and down the kingdom. This legislative surgery-cum-midwifery resulted not only in the amputation of large slices of north Somerset and south Gloucestershire to bring to birth the new county of Avon, but also in the total eradication of the *county* of Bristol, which had enjoyed independent status from the counties of Somerset and Gloucestershire since 1373. Bristol ("the birthplace of America") is now merely one of six 'districts' of Avon. The Roman city of Bath, formerly in Somerset, is another.

Happily, apart from giving this book an 'honest' title, we are not concerned with demarcation lines drawn by pundits of the 1970s. The book is about people of the past and the effect their lives had upon their times and upon subsequent history. The original counties of Somerset and of Bristol, with those parts of south Gloucestershire which, being in Avon, come within the scope of this book, are particularly rich in historical personalities and associations far beyond their borders, notably America and Australia. Those were the days when Avon had only one meaning: that of a tidal river, dividing Somerset and Gloucestershire, down the gorge of which sailed explorers and merchant venturers to distant and often unknown lands.

April 1978

C.W.

CONTENTS AND ILLUSTRATIONS

BIBLIOGRAPHY

Dictionary of National Biography, (Oxford University Press)

King Edgar, Helen Panter (Morgan Books, Bath)

Inside Somerset, Monica Hutchings (Abbey Press, Sherborne)

Portrait of Somerset, Bryan Little (Robert Hale, 1969)

Somerset, Ralph Whitlock (Batsford, 1975)

Sedgemoor and Avalon, Desmond Hawkins (Robert Hale, 1974)

A Thousand Lives, Iris Morley (Andre Deutsch)

Portrait of Bristol, Keith Brace (Robert Hale, 1969)

Portrait of Exmoor, J. H. B. Peel (Robert Hale, 1970)

The Bristol Story, Max Barnes (Bristol United Press, 1973)

Trajectus Augusti

AUST

Ever since the Roman "out to Severn strode", Aust has been the scene of historic achievements in methods of river-crossing. Sabrina was the charming name they gave to the river Severn and to reach the Welsh shore of its estuary they worked a ferry which they called Trajectus Augusti. It was a formidable task. The tides run at a speed of nine knots, their rise-and-fall exceeds forty feet and at certain seasons a hefty tidal bore roars up towards Gloucester. Timing of the crossing was all-important, and remained so for centuries after the Legions had left Britain.

Vehicles as large as stage-coaches were ferried across the Old Passage, to and from Aust and Beachley, on the western bank. It was superseded by the New Passage, downstream, in the 19th-century. With the coming of railways an underwater crossing was achieved: the Severn Tunnel, built by the Great Western Railway, its entrance between Aust and Bristol, was completed in 1866 and gave direct access between London and South Wales.

The latter-day Roman ferry was in use for pedestrians and road vehicles until the magnificent and delicate Severn Bridge was opened by the Queen in 1966. It spans two rivers, the Severn to the Beachley peninsula, which it crosses, and continues over the Welsh river Wye, fulfilling a dream of 140 years, since Thomas Telford, the celebrated 19th-century bridge builder, first proposed a suspension bridge there in 1824.

It forms a section of the M4 motorway and is the lightest bridge for its length and loading ever built.

King John's Hunting Lodge

AXBRIDGE

Snugly beneath the north-western edge of the Mendip Hills lies ancient Axbridge, a base for what was once the royal Chase known as Mendip Forest. When the Normans came, ferocious forest laws were codified and applied, on the lines of the better-known royal hunting preserves of the New Forest in Hampshire.

Medieval kings, with their passion for hunting, gave Axbridge considerable status, but of all the Norman and subsequent Plantagenet monarchs who came there for sport King John is most remembered. There, in a central position facing the main square is a building traditionally known as King John's Hunting Lodge – and the site of a similar retreat once occupied by his Saxon predecessors.

The building is an early Tudor merchant's house. Now a National Trust property, it contains a museum of local history and archaeology. The oldest existing building in Axbridge is its noble 15th-century church with a fine tower, standing on an eminence overlooking the parish.

The rigorous forest laws of Mendip gradually fell into desuetude after the Middle Ages but Charles I, with characteristic inability to adapt to changing times, tried to revive the obsolete royal prerogative. It was not until the accession of William and Mary that the laws were finally abandoned.

A terrible blow was suffered by Axbridge – and nearby villages – on a spring day in 1973. A large 'plane-load of its womenfolk set off on a one-day outing to Switzerland. The aircraft crashed near Basle, with appalling loss of life.

BADMINTON

Played by men and women world-wide, the game of badminton takes its name from the Duke of Beaufort's country seat at Badminton although the sport, played with racquets and shuttlecocks, originated in India. Its rules were compiled at Poona in 1876 and formed the basis of an English set drawn up some years later by the Bath Badminton Club. All-England championships were first held in 1899.

Badminton House, a 17th-century mansion incorporating parts of an older building, is the focal point of what is sometimes affectionately nicknamed "Beaufortshire". It is a district dedicated to the Horse, though for those whose interests are purely aesthetic the house itself, with its collection of old master paintings and Grinling Gibbons wood-carving, is open to the public on one afternoon weekly during summer months.

But around Badminton the Horse is paramount. The renowned Beaufort Hunt covers a lovely undulating Cotswold countryside and in recent years have been held the gruelling Badminton Horse Trials – the 'Three-Day Event' – attracting thousands of spectators, including the Queen, and a formidable array of riders, among whom have been Princess Anne.

The master of Badminton, Henry Hugh Arthur Fitzroy Somerset, tenth Duke of Beaufort, was born in 1900 and succeeded his father in 1924. He held an ancient – and highly appropriate – office in the Royal Household, third in seniority after those of the Lord Chamberlain and the Lord Steward.

From 1936 until 1978 the Duke was Master of the Horse.

BATH

Before the Christian era a princely but leprous swineherd discovered the healing hot mineral springs at the place now known as Bath.

He was Prince Bladud, only son of Lud Hudibras, king of the Britons. The young prince contracted leprosy, causing him to be banished from court. During his wanderings he got a job as a swineherd, but his porcine charges also contracted the disease.

In the Avon valley where Bath now stands there was a boggy morass, bubbling with hot springs. Bladud's swine wallowed in it and after a period of such daily baths their scales began to fall away. So the prince himself tried out the treatment, taking regular muddy plunges, until eventually both prince and pigs were cured. He had quartered himself and his herd nearby at Swineswick (now Swainswick) and the only feature of the landscape which he could recognise today is eastwards to Little Solsbury hill. Before his time it had been, on its plateau, an Iron Age village but the site was abandoned about 100 B.C. and has never since been a 'built-up area': it is now in the care of the National Trust.

Bladud, the first patient to 'take the Bath waters', returned to court. He proved an enlightened prince and on succeeding Lud as king he returned to the hot springs, made water-cisterns, erected houses and a palace and there established his capital, naming it Caerbren.

At the top of the Broad Street of Georgian Bath the swineherd-prince is recalled in a short terrace of houses facing the old road to London: Bladud Buildings.

Little Solsbury Hill

BATH

When the Romans came to Bath they named it Aquae Sulis. It was an adroit political move because the native population then worshipped Sul (the sun-god) and resentment towards their new masters would be soothed by the bestowal of the title of 'The Waters of Sul'. The Roman goddess of healing was Minerva, and the temple they erected at Bath was tactfully called that of Sul-Minerva.

They brought Roman practicality, efficiency and skill to harness and develop the hot springs which had brought relief to Prince Bladud and his swine, creating a healing and entertainment centre around the source of the 500,000 gallons of radioactive water which bubbled up daily at a temperature of some 120 degrees Farenheit.

After draining the area and channelling the water into a reservoir to feed a series of baths, they built a magnificent establishment. It included a series of dry-heated 'hypocaust' rooms – sauna baths – heated from flues in walls and under floors.

The dramatic and remarkably complete remains of this great achievement – a spa for healing, relaxing, gossiping, consulting the gods at the adjoining temple – can be seen today. Mineral water still fills the lead-bottomed rectangular Great Bath. Among exhibits are brooches and other items of Roman women's jewellery.

Even a leaden pipe, revealing a plumber's jointing, remains *in situ* alongside the Great Bath, set at an angle at the corner of which is a stone. It was the jumping-off place from which naked Roman swimmers plunged into the warm water: its centre is worn into a curve made by the feet of countless Romans who used it.

BATH

After some four centuries of imperial occupation of Britain the Roman legions were withdrawn about the year 400 A.D. and England became a battleground of warring Anglo-Saxon kingdoms. Political unification came at last and its reality was endorsed at Whitsuntide, 973, in Bath.

At the spot where the Abbey now stands the Wessex King Edgar was anointed and crowned first king of all England, the united provinces of Wessex, Mercia and Northumbria. This enlightened ruler, a patron and protector of the church had become king of England north of the Thames when only fourteen and after the death of his brother Edwig in 959 he was *de facto* ruler of all England for fourteen years before his coronation at Bath made him king *de jure* when he was twenty-nine. He died two years afterwards.

The solemn consecration at Bath set a precedent in anointing and crowning which has not changed substantially to this day. It raised monarchical status by making it an essentially ecclesiastical occasion.

A suggested explanation of this early binding of monarchy and church – the anointed of God and protector of the English Church – after Edgar had ruled so long before his crowning was made by Sir Frank Stenton in his scholarly *Anglo-Saxon England:* . . . . it is probably something more than mere coincidence that the year of his coronation was the year in which he reached the age of thirty, below which no one could be canonically ordained to the priesthood.

The King's Bath

BATH

The Roman baths, not uncovered until modern times, are on the lowest of three levels. Above them came the medieval city (a section of its embattled walls still survives) and on the top layer of the three-decker 'sandwich' is the elegant Georgian Pump Room, on the present street-level. As early as the 12th-century sick and poor people came from afar to bathe and Prince Bladud would be gratified to know that one bath was set aside for the treatment of leprosy.

The fashion of going to Bath really boomed in the 17th-century, set by female royal visitors who believed that total immersion increased chances of fertility. There was at least one grateful patient, for in due course Mary of Modena, wife of James II, gave birth to a son. (He became the Old Pretender).

On 14 June, 1668, Samuel Pepys sampled a bathe in the King's Bath, setting out from his lodging at four in the morning. "Methinks it cannot be too clean" his Diary tells us, "to go so many bodies together in the same water. Strange to see how hot the water is and in some places the springs so hot as the feet not able to endure, but strange to see, when men and women herein, that live all the season in these waters, they cannot but be parboiled".

Next day Pepys played the tourist: "Up and walked up and down the town . . . and so to the great Church. Here a good organ; but a vain pragmatical fellow preached a ridiculous affected sermon that made me angry. So home, walking round the walls of the city which are good, and the battlements all whole".

BATH

The creation and fame of 18th-century Bath – the loveliest and most historic Georgian city in England – depended mainly on three men: a London architect, a Cornish postmaster and a Welsh gambler.

John Wood, architect, town planner and property developer came to Bath in 1727. The raw material and the finance for his building projects were supplied by wealthy Ralph Allen, who that year had bought the neighbouring stone quarries which were to make the oolite 'Bath Stone' famous. And already in the city was installed Richard (Beau) Nash, Master of the Ceremonies, who had gravitated thence from grammar school in Carmarthen via Jesus College, Oxford and a spell in London. All had died between 1754 and 1764, but Wood was succeeded by his architect son, John Wood the Younger, who carried on his father's work.

The Elder Wood's work included the Royal Crescent – the finest crescent in Europe – Queen Square, where he lived in the house under the central pediment on its north side, a modest town house for Ralph Allen (now a pub) and, on a hill overlooking the city, Allen's magnificent mansion of Prior Park; it is now Prior Park College, the Catholic Public School, founded in 1830.

In Cornwall Allen was a postal employee. When he became Bath's postmaster in 1710 he revolutionised the entire system by introducing the cross-posts, which delivered mail direct instead of everything going through London. Operating them for the government made him a huge fortune. Then he developed the local stone quarries.

North Side Queen Square

The Pump Room

BATH

As Master of Ceremonies, Beau Nash ruled the glittering, gambling and dancing society gathered at Bath with a fearless absolutism. He drew up a list of rules for behaviour and dress, displayed in the Pump Room where, in a niche, his statue stands today.

Oliver Goldsmith (1728-1774) writes of instances which reveal other sides of Nash's character: "The money he got without pain, he gave away without reluctance; and whenever unable to relieve a wretch who sued for assistance, he has been often seen to shed tears. A gentleman of broken fortune standing behind his chair as Nash was playing a game of picquet for £200 and observing with what indifference he won the money, could not avoid whispering to another who stood by 'Heavens, how happy all that money would make me'. Nash, overhearing this, clapp'd the money into his hand and cried 'Go, and be happy'".

Beau Nash also had a keen sense of social responsibility. Collecting money to found the Mineral Water Hospital for poor persons (now the Royal National Hospital for Rheumatic Diseases) he tackled a parsimonious duchess. Goldsmith writes that her Grace told Nash to put down "a trifle" for her, since she had no money with her. The Beau began to count up to 25 guineas from his pocket into his white hat, whereupon the duchess protested that she should die of fright. "Madam" said Nash "you will never die doing good, and if you do it will be the better for you".

BATH

Famous residents of the past abound in Bath. Their dwellings are marked by sixty-nine mural tablets. It was from his house in The Circus that Prime Minister William Pitt, M.P. for Bath, decided to introduce Income Tax and it was from there he sent the future hero of Quebec, General Wolfe, who lived in Trim Street, his commission to take a force to Canada. Clive of India also lived in The Circus and at number 17 the first occupier was Thomas Gainsborough – whose rates came to £4 p.a. It was there that he painted a local lad, Master Jonathan Buttall – the famous "Blue Boy" portrait, now in America. Oliver Goldsmith, the statesman Edmund Burke (M.P. for Bristol) and William Wordsworth are recalled in North Parade, which features in Richard Brinsley Sheridan's play *The Rivals.*

Nelson was a house guest of Sir William and Lady (Emma) Hamilton at 2, Pierrepont Street; at the adjoining house the actor and wit James Quin, rival of David Carrick, died in 1736 and is commemorated in the magnificent Abbey. He described Bath as "a good place for an old cock to roost in". Sarah Siddons lived in The Paragon and commuted between Bath and Bristol for stage appearances each week, for a combined fee of fifty shillings. Admiral Earl Howe, victor in 1794 of "The Glorious First of June" retired to live in Pulteney Street. And in Queen Square dwelt the physician to the Royal Mineral Water Hospital, whose name has won gastronomic immortality: Dr. William Oliver, "inventor" of the renowned biscuit whose centre is embossed with his profile. The wheaten biscuit is universally known simply as a Bath Oliver.

Royal Crescent

BATH

Among the many famous literary figures associated with Bath, three novelists achieved immortality: Henry Fielding, Jane Austen and Charles Dickens.

The Somerset-born author of *The History of Tom Jones, a Foundling,* his masterpiece, was plagued by ill-health and impecuniosity, but he had good friends and patrons, one of whom was Ralph Allen, of Prior Park. He provided lodging and seclusion for Fielding and his sister Sarah (also a novelist) at Widcombe Manor. There Henry wrote much of *Tom Jones,* basing his character of the good Squire Allworthy upon that of philanthropic Ralph Allen.

In 1928 Widcombe Manor became the home of another novelist. Horace Annesley Vachell, author of *The Hill,* the story of life at Harrow, published in 1905. (Incidentally, Fielding had been at Eton). Vachell's best-known work, as a book and a play, was *Quinney's,* published in 1914. Like Jane Austen before him, Vachell was very involved with the niceties of social rank, creating the euphemism "out of the top drawer".

Jane Austen lived for a few years at Sydney Place, off Great Pulteney Street. In her novel *Persuasion* there is a superb "top drawer" account of the snobbish baronet Sir Walter Elliot taking to task his daughter Anne for wishing to visit a widow called Smith ("a mere Mrs. Smith") in the unfashionable Westgate Buildings.

Widcombe Manor

BATH

Charles Dickens when a journalist visited Bath and his observant eye was later to reflect with humour and satire the essence of the spa in the 19th-century, in *Pickwick Papers.*

Very different from the austere Beau Nash was the fictional Master of Ceremonies, Angelo Cyrus Bantam, who welcomed Pickwick and his party to a ball at the Assembly Rooms; he was perky yet obsequious, over-bejewelled, over-scented, perpetually chatting, a slave to hyperbole. The magnificent suite of rooms was designed by John Wood the Younger and completed in 1771. In the present century it suffered decline, but restored to pristine glory by the National Trust in 1938, only to be gutted by fire during an air raid in 1942 – but restored again and re-opened in 1963, since when the building is not only again used as setting for great social occasions but part of it houses an enthralling Museum of Costume.

Mr. Pickwick's servant, Sam Weller, was introduced to mineral waters in the Pump Room by Angelo Cyrus Bantam's footman. It is still possible to taste the mineral water from the fountain in the Pump Room, but most of the daily 500,000 gallons of it runs to waste in the Avon: the adjoining treatment centre was closed in 1976. Latterly, 95 per cent of the patients had been paid for through the National Health Service and that essential source of revenue was withdrawn.

Unless medical and conservationist campaigners succeed in a financial appeal to re-open the old treatment centre, the waters of Britain's last and oldest spa will remain 'redundant'.

Old treatment centre

Church

BATHAMPTON

A place of pious pilgrimage for Australians stands in the quiet village of Bathampton, beside the river Avon less than two miles upstream from Bath. In the church is buried Arthur Phillip, founder of Australia and first Governor of New South Wales.

Admiral Phillip, born in London in 1738, retired to Bath to spend his last years at 19, Bennett Street, near the Assembly Rooms. His burial place was not officially recognised until 1879, when the Government of New South Wales initiated a search in the Bath area.

When Phillip was assigned in 1786 to form a convict settlement in Australia the statesman Viscount Sydney received a less than enthusiastic recommendation for the choice from the great Admiral Lord Howe, who wrote to Sydney: "I cannot say the little knowledge I have of Captain Phillip would have led me to select him for service of this complicated nature". But Howe's snide words were to prove utterly unjustified, for Phillip's energy, self-reliance, humanity and firmness made a lasting impression on New South Wales. And he named Sydney after the man who had shown faith in his ability.

He sailed in the frigate *Sirius,* with the tender *Supply,* and reached Botany Bay on 18 January, 1788. Unsatisfied, he went on to Port Jackson (mentioned by Captain Cook) and pitched the new settlement at the end of that month. He suffered from the lack of voluntary settlers and the danger of starvation was not removed until 1790.

Admiral Phillip's tomb

BATHAMPTON

Privation affected Phillip's health and he returned, sick, to England and obtained permission to resign in August, 1793. He was granted a pension "in considerations of meritorious services" and at Bath his health improved.

Within Bathampton's church of St. Nicholas is the Philip Memorial and Australia Chapel, dedicated in 1975, where the Holy Communion is celebrated every Thursday morning. It is a corner of Australia in rural England.

The Cross and Altar candles were presented by the Australian Government; the screen of Australian Blackbeam wood and other furnishings were given by the Fellowship of First Fleeters, a New South Wales society whose members trace their families back to the first colonizing party in 1788; the original floor was re-laid with Australian Wombeyan marble specially cut and presented by the Hammerston Group of companies; and two windows are blazoned with the armorial bearings and mottoes of the Australian Government and of the six States. And on the marble floor an inscribed memorial balustrade to Arthur Phillip stands behind the original tombstone recording the resting place of the Admiral and of his wife, Isabella.

Also resting in this village church, or its graveyard, is an intriguing medley of late 18th- and early 19th-century notabilities: John Rye (1767-1855) founder in 1839 of the Shipwrecked Mariners' Benevolent Society; Sir Roderick Murchison (1798-1871) director of the Geological Survey of the United Kingdom; and Vicomte du Barry, kinsman of Louis XV's famous mistress. He was killed in a duel.

BATHFORD

Moses and Eleazer Pickwick had been proprietors of the White Hart coaching inn at Bath. The quaint surname derives from the fact that Moses was a foundling "picked up at Wick", a nearby village. When Charles Dickens, always on the lookout for unusual names for his fictional characters, visited Bath he spotted the name of Pickwick – and made it immortal. Eleazer Pickwick (1749-1837) is buried at Bathford.

Also interred at Bathford is a young woman with an even more famous name: Ann Nelson. She died age twenty-three, when her brother Horatio was a naval captain, but after his greater fame and a peerage in 1801 a panel was added to her tombstone recording that she was 'sister of Viscount Nelson' – a delicious example of posthumous 'one-upmanship'.

Flighty Ann Nelson (an unmarried mother) followed the prevailing fashion when attending a ball at Bath. Her ankle-length dress had been deliberately made damp, so as to cling to her figure revealingly. But, doubtless like other young women of her period, she paid a high price for the sexy fashion.

She died of pneumonia.

BRENDON HILLS

A few miles to the south-west of Watchet the gentle range of the Brendon Hills gives an introduction to the more austere, virtually treeless beauty of Exmoor to the westward and to the twisting boundary where Somerset meets Devon. Indeed, the charming village of Brendon, in the steep vale watered by the East Lyn river on its way to join its West Lyn brother before finding the sea at Lynmouth Bay, in fact belongs to the latter county. Its attractive inn is aptly named "The Staghunters" for it is in an area favoured for meets of the "Devon and Somerset".

Now so rural, the Brendon Hills have a long history which curiously manages to link the Bronze Age with the Industrial Revolution; and between those thousands of years there is ample evidence that the ancient Britons established themselves there.

In the hills, Bronze Age man, who may be credited with discovering metal and its uses, had the raw material under their feet: the shelly limestone contained veins of carbonate of iron.

Traversing the Brendons today, it needs a very vivid imagination to regard the range of hills as a place also comparatively modern, humming with the production of iron ore. Yet in the 19th-century parts of the area were agog with activity: the iron ore workings were exploited by a South Wales company at Ebbw Vale, to feed the hungry furnaces.

BRIDGWATER

Since it became a chartered borough almost 800 years ago, Bridgwater has played a part, both directly and indirectly, in many historic events, but its fame is mainly associated with the name of Admiral Robert Blake; he was born there in 1598 and as Oliver Cromwell's "General-at-Sea" was to give his country naval supremacy.

The town lies on either side of the river Parrett, which flows into the Bristol Channel near the mouth of the Severn. In 1295 it returned two members to Parliament and in 1468 Edward IV gave it the right to have a Mayor. Its quaysides were busy exporting westcountry cloth and importing wine.

Its name commemorates the fact that its early wooden bridge provided an important crossing from the low-lying marshy moorland to the east, though the second part of the name does not refer to water, but to Walter: the bridge named after the 11th-century Walter of Douai. When the Bridge of Walter became abbreviated to Bridgwater it lost its 'e', although that vowel is retained in the town's flattering galaxy of namesakes: at least thirteen of them in two Continents.

Bridgewater, Massachusetts, was incorporated in 1656, though there is no evidence in Bridgwater's records that the original settlers hailed from the English town.

Several westcountry place-names, not unnaturally, in view of the Puritan exodus, are reproduced in Massachusetts and the Bridgewater in that State is in Plymouth County, some ten miles from Taunton, Mass. – about the same distance apart as are the two Somerset towns.

BRIDGWATER

Terrible punishment was unnecessarily suffered by the townsfolk and town in the Civil War, which the Royalists had already virtually lost when they were routed at Naseby under Sir Thomas Fairfax, with Oliver Cromwell, in June, 1645.

The Roundheads then moved into Somerset to raise the siege of Taunton, which Robert Blake had long been defending with terrifying tenacity. They closed in on Bridgwater, whose ordinary inhabitants were almost to a man the staunch supporters of the Parliament. But the town's castle was a Royalist stronghold, well supplied with ammunition and rich with treasure which the local gentry had stored there for safe-keeping.

Sir Edmund Wyndham, the castle's Governor, rejected a summons to surrender when Fairfax and Cromwell came in person before the walls. The Roundheads began their attack at night. For three days the batteries of both castle and besiegers turned the town into a ruinous inferno. The townpeoples' pleas to the Governor to surrender went unheeded, although a truce was called to evacuate women and children.

Eventually Fairfax (who was senior to Cromwell in command) offered Governor Wyndham quarter for the lives of the garrison, and Sir Edmund formally surrendered. The Roundheads seized the rich booty within the castle – then destroyed its defences.

It happened in the year that Bridgwater-born Robert Blake, then a colonel in the Roundhead army and defender of Taunton castle, was a Member of Parliament for his native town.

Farmhouse near Bridgwater

Robert Blake

BRIDGWATER

The statue of Robert Blake stands in imposing isolation on the forecourt of Cornhill, in the heart of the older part of the town on the western side of the river Parrett. The image matches the man: truculent, commanding and shatteringly grim of visage.

Blake was twice Bridgwater's Member of Parliament but it was as a warrior by land and sea that he won lasting fame. On the outbreak of the Civil War he distinguished himself in defending Bristol against the King's forces and took and held Taunton, where his doggedness is explicit in his reply to a summons to surrender the castle after a year-long siege: "we are resolved to the last drop of our blood to maintain the quarrel we have undertaken".

After the execution of Charles I, Cromwell set about building a navy from the nucleus of the Commonwealth's ships and it was Blake who put the fleet to devastating use. He chased Prince Rupert's royalist vessels resolutely, all the way to the Mediterranean. The austere and pertinaceous Puritan captured the Royalist-held Scilly Islands. With a now powerful Commonwealth fleet he successfully challenged and finally obliterated the naval supremacy of the Dutch Republic after war broke out in 1652, suffering only one defeat in a series of brilliant engagements up and down the English Channel. By 1655 he was again in the Mediterranean, destroying the notorious Barbary pirates on the North Africa coast, boldly sailing under the batteries at Porto Farino and burning their fleet.

Blake's Museum

BRIDGWATER

Blake's final feat, in 1657, was probably his most brilliant. Although he was a sick man – he had been badly wounded in action against the Dutch five years earlier – he attacked Santa Cruz, the port of Teneriffe in the Canary Islands. Sailing in under a crescent of forts which he silenced one by one, he utterly annihilated the Spanish treasure fleet.

History knows him as Admiral Blake, though that rank was not used when he was appointed "General-at-Sea". He applied his military training to tactics afloat, completely altering the English methods of seaborne attack. But it was not alone to his new ideas in naval warfare that he owed his historic achievements. The touchstone of his rugged genius was his utter confidence in his own powers, his tenacity of purpose, his passionate belief in the Commonwealth's cause, and in consequence the hold over his men, who would follow him into any enterprise.

In an unobtrusive street in the heart of Bridgwater (predictably now called Blake Street) is a comparatively modest house which is his putative birthplace. It houses the excellently staged Blake Museum.

It does not deal exclusively with the Admiral, for the museum also abounds in items of the history of the town and district, including the event which brought it tragic fame twenty-eight years after Blake's death: the last days of the Monmouth Rebellion, culminating in the Battle of Sedgemoor, some three miles away.

BRIDGWATER

The Blake museum contains portraits and some possessions of three ancient Somerset families, those of Alford, Symes and Sydenham. Their ancestry dates back beyond the Middle Ages, though they are more relevant to Somerset's history from the 16th-century, when they dwelt respectively at Westonzoyland, near Bridgwater; Pitminster, outside Taunton; and Brympton d'Evercy, a couple of miles from Yeovil. In the 18th-century the three families became interwoven by the marriages of John Symes, a Bridgwater doctor, and Richard Symes, a lawyer, respectively to Susannah Coles, of a branch of the Alfords, and to Elizabeth Sydenham. The Alfords were west country landowners at the time of the Conquest, but their most significant member was a 17th-century man.

He was Gregory Alford, and he played a key part in the subsequent history of the monarchy on a June day in 1685, when he was Mayor of the little Dorset port of Lyme.

The Duke of Monmouth, with an 'invasion force' of only eighty fully armed men from three small ships, landed at Lyme, set up headquarters at the George inn and started recruiting.

Mayor Alford, with a couple of companions, slipped away to Honiton, where he wrote a letter to King James II. Alford's companions rode with it to London.

His Majesty was quick to despatch the pick of his army to the west-country, with disastrous consequences to Monmouth. A photo-copy of Alford's vital tip-off letter can be seen in the Blake Museum at Bridgwater.

Castle Street

BRIDGWATER

The exceptionally high and graceful spire of St. Mary's Church, rising from a battlemented tower, dates from 1367. It was from the vantage point of the tower that the Duke of Monmouth examined, through a "perspective glass", the flat expanse of Sedgemoor a few hours before his motley army made the disastrous attack on the King's forces which marked the end of the Monmouth Rebellion.

The Church is lovingly cared for by the parishioners and in recent years has been the scene of ambitious festivals of music and the arts. Among its treasures is perhaps the finest painting in any church within the country. It depicts the Descent from the Cross and was given in 1783 by the Hon. Anne Paulet (he was named after Queen Anne) who had become Bridgwater's Member of Parliament in 1768.

Nothing remains of the castle, but on its site between St. Mary's Church and the quayside on the west bank of the river Parrett is the early Georgian gem of Castle Street, leading out of a tranquil square and isolated from the town's busy shipping zone.

Castle Street owes its existence to the Duke of Chandos, one of those rich magnates who embellished the 18th-century with magnificence and enterprise. He bought the lordship of the manor in 1721 and set out to develop Bridgwater to rival Bristol's great status as a trading port. His ambitious scheme failed, but the merchants' and harbour officials' houses in Castle Street fortunately remain intact.

St. Mary's Church

BRIDGWATER

When the Monmouth Rebellion had been crushed and the detested Judge Jeffreys had done his ruthless work, the unpopular King James felt safe enough to visit Bridgwater in 1686. But by 1688 he had fled his kingdom and the Protestant William of Orange had landed. That event fermented enthusiasm in Bridgwater for celebrating the Fifth of November, 1605 – in the reign of James's grandfather.

Thousands come to the town each year on the Thursday nearest to Guy Fawkes Day, to witness an astonishing series of events. They start with a procession of illuminated *tableaux vivants* through the streets after dark, each "float" depicting some colourful historical scene, not necessarily relating to the town's history, nor to any particular period.

The silent procession of static figures is followed by a noisy one of highly animated and vocal participants – a series of "features", with loud music and singing, and non-stop dancing.

After the processions there is an interval, while the "Gangs" assemble in groups in High Street for the town's most spectacular speciality, the "squibbing" display. Each man carries a long wooden handle with a Bridgwater Squib attached to the business end. When ignited the squibs are held aloft over the competitors' heads and as each firework burns out it shoots a star high into the air. Scores of these formidable squibs – measuring two and a half inches in bore and about eighteen inches long – are discharged.

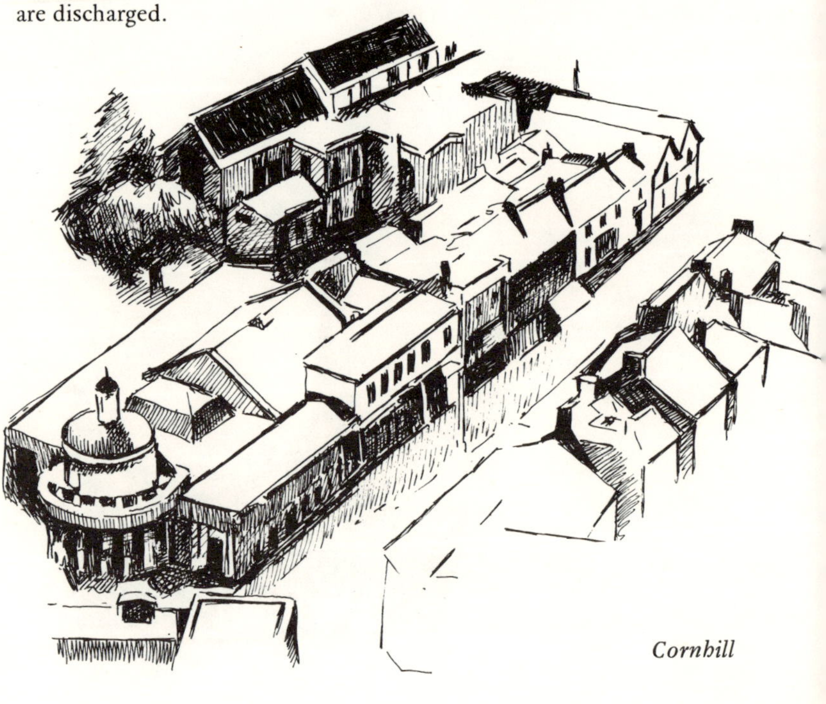

Cornhill

BRISTOL

Bristol may justly claim to be the birthplace of America, whose very name almost certainly derives from a senior Bristol official, Richard Ameryke.

John Cabot, a Venetian who had settled in Bristol, was given authority by the shrewd and commercially-minded Welshman, Henry VII, to seek out territories "hitherto unknown to all Christians". With his son Sebastian and a crew of eighteen, in the 100-ton ship *Matthew* he set sail in May, 1497, from Bristol's Quayside, down the Avon gorge to the Severn and away across the Atlantic. He made his first landfall in what is now Nova Scotia, then sailed north to Newfoundland.

Cabot had been preceeded across the Atlantic by Christopher Columbus, but Columbus had been seeking a westward passage to India; he did not discover the mainland, but found a group of islands – hence the name West Indies.

On 24 June, 1497, Cabot disembarked and hoisted the English flag, claiming the 'new found land' for the king.

On his triumphant return to Bristol he received payment on the king's behalf from the hands of Richard Ameryke; what is more credible than as a compliment to his paymaster, Cabot should have given his discovery the name of Ameryka?

Cabot went to court to give the king his own account of finding the New World, and was granted £10 from the royal privy purse. Later, Henry VII bestowed upon him a pension of £20 a year – payable out of the revenues of the port of Bristol's Customs, of which department the chief officer was Richard Ameryke.

Cabot sails to discover America

Neptune at Quayhead

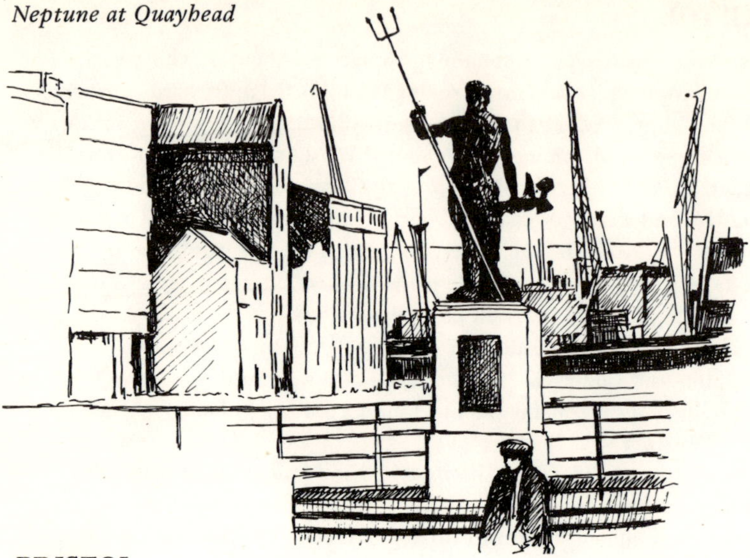

BRISTOL

More than a century before Cabot's time Bristol was a flourishing commercial centre, as it still remains. By 1373 its importance was such that Edward III granted a charter to create it an autonomous county. It was the first provincial town to acquire the status and it remained the City and County of Bristol for 600 years. But in 1974 local government reorganisation caused its demotion; with the creation of the County of Avon the city is simply one of the Districts within that new county.

Maritime trade was the foundation of Bristol's prosperity and its guild of merchants, whose venturing had opened up sea routes for trade and who were jealous of inefficient interlopers using the port obtained a charter from Edward VI in 1552. In the present Hall of the Society of Merchant Venturers of Bristol, at Clifton Down, the document is displayed. Elizabeth I, Charles I and Charles II confirmed the Merchant Venturers' considerable powers by granting fresh charters.

The Society now acts as trustee for educational and other charitable foundations and from its own funds it subscribes annually to more than 200 locally based charities.

By the 18th-century Bristol had become the second city in the kingdom. Ship-owning merchants made large fortunes, in particular from the slave trade; they did not buy and sell slaves, but were their transporters from Africa to America – in appallingly over-crowded and barbaric conditions. It was a triangular traffic, the ships returning to Bristol with cargoes, notably rum, tobacco and sugar from the plantations in the colonies of the New World.

BRISTOL

Edward Colston is Bristol's most celebrated and respected son. He was born there in 1636 and became a great merchant, trading mostly with the West Indies, and was Member of Parliament for his native city from 1710-1713.

He amassed a large fortune and put it to good use, for he was a philanthropist in the grand manner. Schools and almshouses in the city still bear his name, which is also commemorated in Colston Avenue (where his status stands) and in Colston Hall, the large concert hall whose building also incorporates a theatre. When he founded and endowed Colston's School in 1708 he appointed the Merchant Venturers' Society as sole managers of the estates of the charity. He lived in Small Street, inside the walls of the old medieval city and is buried at All Saints church, nearby.

Colston's constructive benevolence was emulated after his death in 1721 by no fewer than three separate Colston societies, meeting at subscription banquets on his birthday, 13 November. One of them, the Dolphin Society, was so named after the dolphin forming part of Colston's armorial bearings.

Some years before his death, Colston gave definite instructions about his funeral: "I would not have the least pomp used at it".

But Bristolians disregarded the wish of their city's greatest benefactor. The bedecked funeral cavalcade, witnessed by young and old in thousands, was a great occasion – the epitome of 18th-century pomp and funereal splendour.

Colston's House

BRISTOL

John Wesley's "New Room" in the Horsefair is a centre of world pilgrimage. It was there that the founder of Methodism lived and from there he began his open-air preaching tours. His brother Charles, the hymn writer, became pastor and preacher in the chapel, the first Methodist chapel in the world and still constantly in use. It has an elegant interior, with Doric columns and two staircases flanking a double pulpit, one immediately above the other. In the courtyard is a fine commemorative equestrian statue of John Wesley, whose horses's stable adjoined the main building.

A frail man of indomitable will, Wesley was born in 1703, the fifteenth of nineteen children of a Lincolnshire rector. From his ordination as an Anglican priest in 1728 until the end of his long life he rose at 4 a.m. daily. It was owing to the strict ordering of his life, and that of his brother, in their Oxford days that they were derisively nicknamed "Methodists".

In 1735 the Wesley brothers were sent by the Society for the Propagation of the Gospel to America, establishing headquarters at Savannah, in the colony of Georgia, and the first Methodist chapel was opened in New York in 1784 – eight years after American Independence.

In Wesley's time the Established church was in a state of lethargy, deploring enthusiasm, and the various forms of Nonconformity were narrow, politically minded and sectarian. Of the eighteen Methodist conferences held in the 18th-century at Wesley's New Room in Bristol the first, in 1774, marked the irreparable break with the Anglicans.

Wesley's New Room

BRISTOL

"The fairest, goodliest and most famous parish church in England". Thus was St Mary Redcliffe described by Elizabeth I when she visited Bristol in 1574. Few (and certainly no Bristolian) would challenge her Majesty's assessment for the church is generally accepted as England's finest example of extant Gothic architecture.

Redcliffe is the trans-Avon part of the original city and there was great rivalry between "the men of Bristol and the men of Redcliffe". In the 15th-century the great merchants lived there and William Canynges was the richest of them all. His money ensured the restoration of this parish church after the spire had been struck by lightning in 1446. The merchant prince later entered the priesthood.

Within, the church presents in its monuments an historical pageant from medieval times to the present day, including American associations. The rib of a cow-whale brought to the church by John and Sebastian Cabot after discovering the American continent at Newfoundland. The armour and ships' pennants of Admiral Sir William Penn with an epitaph recording his career, composed by his son, the Quaker William Penn, founder of Pennsylvania.

And the chapel of St. John the Baptist, now known as the American Chapel. It was restored and furnished by the Friends of St. Mary Redcliffe in the United States. The kneelers, worked by individual Friends, depict the arms of the thirteen original States and the seven original dioceses and the service books were the gift of the Welcome Society of Pennsylvania.

St. Mary Redcliffe

BRISTOL

England's oldest theatre which has been continually in use (with but a few short breaks) since 1776 is the Theatre Royal in King Street. Its foundation was vigorously opposed by local Puritanical lobbyists who argued that the playhouse would risk the morals of the city's youth, seduce the innocent and "diffuse an habit of idleness, indolence and debauchery". The blasphemous use of "Gad" for God and the simulation of passionate love, often adulterous, were among other objections.

From 1776 until the latter part of the 19th-century, when decline set in, almost every famous actor and actress performed at the Theatre Royal except Garrick, though he admired the place and wrote the prologue and epilogue for the opening. Two world wars played havoc with the theatre's fortunes and in 1942 it was put up for auction. But Bristolians, backed by the Arts Council and other organisations, saved it. In 1946 the London 'Old Vic' theatre sent a residential company – the Bristol Old Vic. It started a revival which was dramatic in both senses.

In recent years the Theatre Royal has extended and blossomed. The large but obsolete Coopers' (barrel-makers') Hall, adjoining the somewhat dingy theatre entrance, is now part of the theatre complex. It not only provides a worthy entrance and spacious foyer, but the expansion scheme has also enabled the Theatre Royal to become the home of the Bristol Old Vic Theatre School, its amenities including a students' studio theatre and administrative quarters above. The School works in association with Bristol University's Drama department.

BRISTOL

The church of the dissolved St. Augustine's Abbey, founded in 1140, became at the Reformation the cathedral of the new diocese of Bristol in 1542. In the precincts is the Cathedral School, descendent of the ancient monastic school. Paramount among the early architecture which remains is one of the finest Norman rooms in England, the magnificent Chapter House, which came near to destruction during the Reform Riots of 1831.

Among the memorials in the Cathedral are some which recall Bristol's great era of merchant venturing, notably a pair of Roman-style silver candlesticks dated 1712. They were given by John Rumsey, the Town Clerk, as a thank-offering for the safe return from a round-the-world voyage of two ships, *The Duke* and *The Duchess,* a venture in which Rumsey had a big stake.

The expedition was commanded by Woodes Rogers, a privateering Bristolian and called at the uninhabited island of Juan Fernandez. There he rescued and brought back to Bristol Alexander Selkirk, who had been deliberately marooned by a sea-captain with whom he had quarrelled. When Daniel Defoe heard the story he made Selkirk the prototype for his great tale of adventure, *Robinson Crusoe.*

Another thank-offering, totally different in form and purpose from Rumsey's is a stained glass window of three panels depicting a range of Biblical subjects. After her recovery from sickness it is said to have been given, in 1683, by Nell Gwynn.

Cathedral

BRISTOL

Ex-king James II brought a force of French troops to Ireland – which had "declared" for the Stuart – and was defeated at the Battle of the Boyne in July, 1690, by William III. His Secretary of State for Ireland was Sir William Southwell of Kings Weston, a lovely site overlooking the confluence of the Avon and Severn, near Bristol. The King returned from Ireland in September, stayed overnight at Southwell's house and left for London next day, via Bristol, in the Duke of Beaufort's coach.

Kings Weston was then a Tudor building but in 1710 Sir Robert's son and successor, Edward, built the present house on the site. It was designed by the celebrated and versatile Sir John Vanburgh, who combined his genius for architecture, of which Blenheim Palace is perhaps the best known, with the writing of witty, saucy, sexy plays which are still performed, notably *The Provok'd Wife* and *The Relapse, or Virtue in Danger.* Kings Weston is one of Vanbrugh's smallest buildings and he died before its completion. It is a gem of its kind and although its once open prospect is now enclosed by the suburban buildings of Shirehampton, its interior of fine plasterwork ceilings, 18th-century pictures and a rare 'hanging' staircase, is carefully preserved.

Since 1832, when the last Southwell died without issue, Kings Weston (with its considerable ancillary buildings) has had a varied history. Now Vanbrugh's house, part of which is open to the public during summer months by appointment, is safe for posterity in the hands of the Police: it is a residential training school for officers of the Avon and Somerset Constabulary.

Kings Weston

BRISTOL

Chocolate, tobacco and wine are the three commodities which are historically associated with Bristol's importing and commercial fame. In 1761 the Bristolian Joseph Fry, a Quaker, obtained a patent to manufacture chocolate; another native who in the 1780s started in a small way on the quayside, selling tobacco and snuff to sailors and merchants, laid the foundation of a renowned tobacco industry – his name was Wills; and the families of Avery and of Harvey are indelibly linked with the wines they imported, notably the sherry universally known as "Bristol Milk".

A distinguished native of his time, outside the field of commerce, was Samuel Plimsoll (1824-1898) the social reformer and "Sailors' Friend". Overloading of merchant ships had become a scandal and in 1864 Plimsoll himself nearly lost his life in one such "coffin ship". The now familiar marks on ships' sides to denote the waterline limit to which they could safely be loaded – the Plimsoll Line– had been recommended by the Royal National Lifeboat Institution; but Plimsoll met with less than enthusiasm for a Parliamentary enactment. Members were uninterested because merchant seamen were then second-class citizens, having no vote under the 1867 Reform Act!

A commemorative bust of Samuel Plimsoll stands at the side of the Avon, facing downstream, between the city's old docks and Brunel's suspension bridge at Clifton which spans the Avon Gorge. The site is touchingly appropriate, for the bridge was opened in the very year that Plimsoll's humane campaign was inspired by his personal experience of near-shipwreck in an overloaded "coffin ship".

Samuel Plimsoll

BRISTOL

To Isambard Kingdom Brunel, civil engineer, builder of bridges, docks, tunnels, railways and steamships, Bristol owes much of its 19th-century history. His most spectacular and beautiful achievement is Clifton Suspension Bridge, spanning the Avon Gorge between Bristol and what was then Somerset. His original design was made in 1831, when he was only twenty-five, but the project (open to competition) suffered decades of financial and other melancholoy delays and he did not live to see the bridge opened in 1864, when it was justifiably described as "the wonder of the age". Its total span, measured from the centre of each pier, exceeds 700 feet.

As engineer to the Great Western Railway Company Brunel surveyed and supervised the construction of its route between Bristol and London. The line was opened in 1841 and 1843 saw the last of the horse-drawn mail coaches between the two cities. At Bristol, as well as making dock improvements, Brunel was a ship-builder in the emergent age of steam. His paddle-driven steamship *Great Western* was launched there in 1837 and his epoch-making *Great Britain* (referred to on the next page) was named by the Prince Consort and launched in 1843.

The second half of the 19th-century was rich in other events. Largely through the Society of Merchant Venturers, the splendid area of Clifton and Durdham Down, extending to the edge of the Avon Gorge, was secured as a public open space for ever; Clifton College was founded in 1862; and in 1899 the city's pride was enhanced by the granting of a Lord Mayoralty.

BRISTOL

The world's first ocean-going propeller-driven steamship was Brunel's iron vessel *Great Britain,* built at Bristol to compete with the fast American sailing packets which had dominated the transatlantic passenger service for decades. The six masts fore and aft of her tall funnel were only to be used for sail to *save* fuel when the wind was favourable – surely an indication of the thrifty commercial acumen of Brunel and his sponsors, the Great Western Steamship Company of Bristol.

Although the ship was luxuriously equipped and furnished, passengers had to observe strict and austere rules. Everyone had to rise at 7 a.m. "unless otherwise permitted by the surgeon". Passengers had to roll up their beds, "sweep the deck (including the space under the bottom of the berths) and throw dirt overboard" and "beds to be well shaken and aired on deck".

The ship's subsequent career included twenty years service between England and Australia and twice refitted as a troopship she took men to the Crimean War and to Bombay at the time of the Indian Mutiny. But after 1876 she lost her passenger-carrying rank and was sold, being converted to the indignity of a cargo sailing vessel and eventually lying for fifty years at the Falkland Islands where, after use as a store-ship she was abandoned as a hulk. But the *Great Britain* was rescued in 1970.

A combination of local patriotism, technical ingenuity and princely generosity enabled Brunel's great ship to be towed proudly back, passing under his Suspension Bridge to the very dry dock at Bristol where she was built. The unique example of Bristol's age-old maritime history is now the city's biggest public attraction.

BRISTOL

In February, 1910, when Filton was still a village north of Bristol, Britain's first large-scale company for the manufacture of aircraft – though not, initially, their engines – was founded in a field near his house by George White (later a baronet) and was destined to become world-famous in the history of aeronautics in war and in peace. The Bristol Aeroplane Company's original aircraft was the *Bristol Boxkite.* It was first flown at Filton in July, 1910, and attained a speed of forty miles an hour. The *Boxkite* was the world's first military aircraft.

Improvements and expansion were rapid. During the first World War Filton produced some 3,500 aeroplanes, of which two-thirds were the celebrated *Bristol Fighter.* In 1920 the aero engine department was formed, development continued apace and just before the outbreak of the second World War Filton was the largest single aeronautical unit in the world. Between 1939 and 1945, Bristol military aircraft, notably the *Bulldog, Beaufighter, Brabazon* and *Blenheim* bomber, were produced day and night by 50,000 employees.

Since 1960 (when Filton became part of the British Aircraft Corporation) another historic milestone has been reached in Bristol's story of travel to distant lands. In 1962 the Anglo-French agreement for the *Concorde* project was signed and the first flight of the supersonic jet airliner from Filton was in April, 1969,

By 1978 the *Concorde* was taking passengers to the U.S.A. – a journey made memorable in the 19th-century by Brunel's Bristol-built *Great Britain,* to the continent discovered by John Cabot when he sailed in the *Matthew* from Bristol in 1497.

The Bristol Boxkite

BURRINGTON COMBE

The sylvan beauty of Burrington Combe conceals several of the cavernous 'holes' so characteristic of the Mendip hills. It is a gorge without the awesome grandeur of Cheddar's, and owes its place in hymnological history to a cleft in one of the rocks where a young parson sheltered from a storm in the 18th-century.

Augustus Montague Toplady was born at Farnham in Surrey, educated at Westminster School and Trinity College, Dublin and took Holy Orders. He was a writer of theological books.

Toplady also wrote poems on sacred themes, but it was his visit to Burrington Combe which secured for him a lasting place in Christendom. His well-loved hymn *Rock of Ages,* inspired by his experience during the storm, was first published in *The Gospel Magazine* in 1775, three years before his death at the age of thirty-eight. Since 1951, Burrington Combe's "Rock of Ages" has borne an inscription explaining the derivation of its name's association with Toplady and his famous hymn.

It is a revered spot, and an ecumenical one. For example, in the summer of 1977 a great open-air service was conducted there. It was addressed by the Bishop of Bath and Wells; the collection was jointly for Christian Aid and the Queen's Silver Jubilee appeal; and music for the hymn-singing was provided by the Salvation Army Band from Bristol. One likes to think that the spirits of Augustus Toplady and John Wesley were among the worshippers – all acrimony forgotten

CASTLE CARY

"I read prayers this morning at C. Cary, it being K. Charles' Martydom. Papa gave me a large cheese . . ."

Thus the historic and domestic run together in the diary of Parson James Woodforde (1740-1802) under the date of 30 January, 1766. His father was rector of nearby Ansford and vicar of Castle Cary, of which James held the curacies for some years until becoming rector of a Norfolk parish. His diaries, kept assiduously, reveal an intimate picture of 18th-century rural England.

Castle Cary has had no effective castle since Plantagenet days; all that remains are its bracken-clad foundations. The second part of its name derives from the river Cary.

Although he was a conscientious and compassionate pastor, Woodforde was also a *bon viveur.* He writes of attending such events as a Play at the Court House at Cary with a large party and records that "the Company was greatly disturbed . . . by the noise of an insolent, saucy mob on the outside of the Play House".

By the time when the diarist had settled in Norfolk, Cary possessed an antidote to such deplorable hooliganism. In 1779 a splendid circular stone lock-up with an elegant domed roof was erected in the centre of the town. The Round House, as it is known, is an architectural gem of its kind and stands on an open space flanked by a fine Georgian house, though one doubts whether malefactors would appreciate its virtues, since the interior diameter is only seven feet. In 1894 it was repaired and in 1922 was presented to the parish council by Sir Henry Hoare, Bt, the lord of the manor.

CHARD

From 1285 Chard was a borough with its independent administration. But, like other small towns, it lost that independence under the re-organisation of local government – as from All Fools Day in 1974.

Another significant event in its history was in 1577, when the town was almost obliterated by fire, so none of its buildings are pre-Elizabethan; yet many are good examples of later periods, notably the spacious Town Hall, its frontage of Tuscan columns proudly protruding from the building line of the wide and busy Fore Street which is part of the main (A30) road.

In High Street is a house where dwelt John Stringfellow, "the inventor of the aeroplane". The claim is a fair one, since Stringfellow made a contraption which he exhibited in London in 1868, and it managed to fly the length of the Crystal Palace. For fuel he had to rely on methylated spirit and when he became properly airborne the rush of air blew out the flame. Like other inventors, he was ridiculed and never lived to see his invention mature; but his models are enshrined in the British Museum.

Five years after Stringfellow's London *début* there was born at a neighbouring farmhouse a girl who was to make political history: Margaret Grace Bondfield.

After a talented and energetic career in the then struggling Trade Union movement, Margaret Bondfield entered Parliament in 1923, becoming parliamentary secretary to the Minister of Labour the following year. By 1929, at the age of 56, she was Minister of Labour. And England's first woman Cabinet Minister.

CHEDDAR

To approach the village of Cheddar, down the magnificent Gorge from the Mendip Hills, is to experience a sight of awesome grandeur. The limestone cliffs rise sheer for hundreds of feet above the winding road which was once, we are told, a river. At the bottom of the Gorge are the celebrated caves, and beyond them the village, watered by the little river Yeo, whose source is still untraced.

The skeletal remains of Cheddar's oldest known inhabitant were discovered in 1903; a cave-man who lived there at least ten thousand years ago. His home is now more public – in the excellent museum.

In 1837 George Cox accidentally discovered the first, and smaller, of the two complexes of caves. Then, in 1890, Richard Gough made the greater discovery of a nearby series of fantastic chambers. For eight years he persevered in exploration – at one point blasting through twelve feet of solid rock – and he opened his caves to the public in 1898.

Cheddar Caves must surely rank as one of Nature's most spectacular wonders: the columns of stalactites and stalagmites and the magnificent range of colours against the white limestone, produced by minerals in the water slowly seeping during aeons of time. Gough's Caves extend, for the visitor, for more than 400 yards from the entrance and in 1976 a new cave tunnel, 270 feet in length, was excavated.

This pre-historic wonderland at the lower end of the Gorge attracts more than a million visitors each year. Necessarily, the vicinity swarms with the concomitants of modern, large-scale tourism. Yet about a mile away, at the head of the flat and fertile vale, is the tranquil and historic Cheddar itself.

The Gorge

CHEDDAR

Cheese has made the name of Cheddar known world-wide and its imitations are now so universal that the word is no longer an indication of origin but has become in effect merely a loosely descriptive adjective. Yet the original Cheddar cheese – still made locally and available complete with its covering of cheese-cloth – has a long history.

A good customer for it was King Henry II. In 1170 he bought a consignment of eighty hundredweight of it, and described it as "the best in England".

Another notable compliment was paid to it, in the 18th-century, by Daniel Defoe, the forthright and observant journalist and pamphleteer. His visit to Cheddar in 1772 reveals that cheese-making was then carried on under a scheme which we would now call a co-operative. The cows, though individually owned, were grazed as a communal herd.

Defoe then explains that the milk went away each day to a central place where every cow-keeper's contribution was measured and recorded before being added to the common stock, for "making one cheese, and no more, so that the cheese is bigger, or less, as the cows yield more, or less, milk, By this method the goodness of the cheese is preserved and, without all dispute, it is the best cheese that England affords, if not that the whole world affords".

But cheese was not Cheddar's only product in Defoe's time. The river Yeo, emerging from the Gorge, supplied power for no fewer than thirteen mills for the grinding of corn and the making of paper.

River Yeo

CHEDDAR

Romans, Saxons and Normans knew Cheddar. The Romans shipped thence, via the rivers Yeo and Axe to a Severn port near Weston-super-Mare, minerals from their mines on Mendip.

It was a royal manor in Alfred the Great's time and is mentioned in his will. It was thrice an assembly point for Wessex witanegamots – in 941, 956 and 968. At the Norman Conquest William I allotted three portions of the manor to his followers – but being a keen hunting man he retained for himself the great Forest of Mendip!

King John (son of Henry II, who gave such a good "plug" to Cheddar cheese) sold the manor to the archdeacon of Wells in 1204. John's son and successor, Henry III, granted Cheddar a charter in 1253 for holding a weekly market and an annual fair.

The dignified 15th-century stepped market cross, its column rising from an octagonal base, was a preaching cross. About a century after its erection it was surrounded by an elegant colonnade of six arches and a battlemented roof, thus providing a dry market for itinerant merchants offering their wares. For that amenity they paid rent to the parish church nearby.

The most socially significant of Cheddar's buildings is a long rectangular house associated with the religious writer, educationist and philanthropist Hannah More (1745-1833). She was a practical social campaigner for improving the religious and educational standards of Mendip's rural folk. Touched by the ignorance and distress which she found at Cheddar, she founded the first day school there in 1789.

CHIPPING SODBURY

This attractive small town to the north east of Bristol has had a long history and retains a strong Cotswold flavour. The church bears some evidence of the 13th- and 14th-centuries and its splendid carved stone canopied pulpit is reached by steps from a pillar in the nave. It is fashionable to deplore 19th-century restorations of ancient churches but we must be grateful to one restorer of the period: George Edmund Street (builder of London's Law Courts) for he re-discovered and restored the pulpit, one of the most outstanding in England, in 1869.

Chipping Sodbury, however, enjoys a claim to world fame through – cricket! At the upper end of the attractive High Street, since re-named Broad Street, is a large old house (now an hotel) set at a right-angle to the building line, looking down upon the town. It was there that Dr. William Gilbert Grace (1848-1915) practised as a "physician and accoucheur". But cricket was his passion.

W. G. Grace came of a local cricketing family. His father and three brothers were well-known players and he appeared in first-class matches when only fifteen. A few years later he was skippering the Gloucestershire County XI. "W.G." captained England in Test Matches against Australia, taking teams there in 1873 and 1891.

By 1900, when his first-class career ended, he had scored more than 54,000 runs – an immense total on the much rougher wickets of his time. His 126 three-figure innings remained a record until broken by Jack Hobbs in 1925. In the 1871 season he totted up ten innings of more than a century and his highest score in first-class cricket was 344.

CLAVERTON

A young man of twenty-three who was to become a statesman of world renown attended a meeting at Claverton Manor on a July day in 1897, and there he made his first political speech.

He was Winston Leonard Spencer Churchill, who was elected Conservative Member of Parliament for Oldham three years after that political *début;* Liberal M.P. for a Manchester constituency in 1906 (having disagreed with his former Party's policy of Tariff Reform); held offices in Asquith's government, becoming First Lord of the Admiralty at the outbreak of the 1914-18 war; and by 1924 had rejoined the Conservatives.

Churchill's mother was an American and it is therefore touchingly appropriate that, since 1961, Claverton Manor has been the American Museum – the only comprehensive museum of Americana in Europe.

The Manor's setting is superb, commanding a rural stretch of the Avon valley, a couple of miles east of Bath. It was designed in 1820 by Jeffrey Wyatville, architect to George IV, and built of Bath stone. It replaced a manorhouse in the village at the foot of the hill, abutting on the Bath-Warminster road. The old manor was besieged and captured by a Parliamentary force in the Civil War.

Claverton's church, rebuilt in the 19th-century, contains the fine tomb of Ralph Allen of Prior Park(1694-1764), the Bath philanthropist, developer of the Bath stone quarries, anti-Jacobite and postal reformer.

Beehive oven

CLAVERTON

Claverton Manor's series of eighteen completely furnished rooms, and other exhibits, provide a staggeringly realistic domestic history of America from the days of the early colonists to the middle of the 19th-century. It enshrines original examples of the development of American craftsmanship and art in furniture, textiles, wall-coverings, needlework, pewterware and utensils. All has come to Claverton from America.

An example of this enthralling historical pageant is a "keeping room", serving a Puritan family as a living and dining room. Its beams and floorboards came from a late 17th-century house in Massachusetts. The room is arranged for a Bible reading by the head of the family whose arm-chair, of almost throne-like proportions, is ready for him at the head of a pedestal table, whereon the Bible lies. The table once belonged to a certain Peregrine White who was born afloat in Cape Cod harbour in 1620 – aboard the *Mayflower*.

Another fascinating domestic touch is the "tavern", with "june ye 21st. 1776" carved on the fireplace lintel – a few weeks before the Declaration of Independence. There, in the beehive oven, American gingerbread is baked today, for visitors.

The grounds, too, are replete with historical interest, notably a replica of the garden of American's first President, George Washington, at Mount Vernon, his Virginia home by the Potomac river. A Somerset family sent him, for the enlargement of his garden, not only plants and seeds, but also a farmer! The octagonal gardenhouse was used as a schoolroom for Washington's step-grandchildren.

The replica of the garden was a gift from the Colonial Dames of America.

CLEEVE ABBEY

It is easy for westbound travellers on the main Bridgwater-Minehead Road to hurry past one of England's Cistercian monastic gems, anciently known as Vallis Florida and approached down a lane east of Washford. There, in the "flowery valley" stand the considerable and exquisite remains of the Abbey of Cleeve, founded towards the end of the 12-century and the only Cistercian abbey in Somerset.

In the following century Henry III granted it "right of wreck" (parts of its estates were washed by the sea) which made a goodly addition to its prosperity. It is recorded that once there was a wrangle between the Abbot and the Sheriff of Devon over the spoils from a Bristol ship which came to grief, when returning from Baltic trading, as far away as Bude Bay, facing the Atlantic.

It was never a populous monastery and at the time of the Dissolution it had (apart from lay brethren) only seventeen monks, but they were reported to the King's Commissioners as being "priests of honest life, who kept good hospitality"; and gave to charity quadruple the average amount for a house of comparable size. But despite pleas from the local gentry it was dissolved.

The estate passed into several lay hands, being sold to the Lutterells of Dunster in 1949. Next year it was re-sold to the Crown and is now happily in the good care of the Department of the Environment, whose lucid and scholarly booklet guides the visitor through the historical and architectural labrynth of this magnificent relic of times past.

Monks' Dormitory

CLEVEDON

In the first rank among the manorial glories of Somerset and the new county of Avon is Clevedon Court, standing well inland from the quiet little seaside resort of Clevedon, which began to be developed as a select watering-place in the early 19-century.

Sir John de Clevedon built the Court in 1320, adding it to an existing tower, and a hall which he adapted into a kitchen. It was used for that purpose until 1957, when it became a museum. The manor later passed through several families.

In 1709 a rich Bristol merchant, Abraham Elton (1654-1727) bought Clevedon Court. A property-owning magnate with interests in Mendip tin-mining, in glass manufacture, in copper and in shipping, he also held high civic offices in Bristol and was made a baronet in 1717.

From the time of his son, Sir Abraham II, the Court began to blossom into elegance, but it was Sir Abraham IV (1718-1790) who gave it much of its "Gothick" touches, in tune with the fashion then emerging from the hitherto prevailing classic style. His son, the fifth baronet, broke with the merchant and civic tradition of the Eltons: he took Holy Orders.

The reverend baronet's intolerance of Dissenters amounted almost to a mania. But his own son, Charles Abraham, ran away with Sarah Smith, the beautiful daughter of a Bristol merchant of known dissenting tendencies. The Reverend Sir Abraham rushed off at full tilt to Bristol, to stop the marriage.

But he was too late.

CLEVEDON

The runaway bridegroom brought poetry and literature to Clevedon Court when he succeeded as sixth baronet in 1842. Sir Charles, a classical scholar with a gift for poetry, was a professional writer. His coterie of friends included Charles Lamb and Robert Southey. William Makepeace Thackeray was often a houseguest and *Henry Esmond* (perhaps his greatest novel) was conceived there and the Lady Castlewood of the book was based upon Elton's youngest daughter.

Julia, Sir Charles Elton's sister, married Henry Hallam, the historian. Their son Arthur, the essayist, died in Vienna and is buried in the Elton vault at St. Andrew's – "Clevedon Old Church" – in a lovely, isolated setting on a cliff-top overlooking the Severn and the Welsh hills.

A deep friendship developed between Arthur Hallam and Alfred Tennyson when they were undergraduates at Trinity College, Cambridge, and Hallam's youthful genius and tragic death in the Austrian capital had a lasting influence on Tennyson's life and thought. It inspired his great elegiac poem, *In Memoriam,* in the course of which he wrote –

The Danube to the Severn gave
The Darken'd heart that beat no more
They laid him by the pleasant shore
And in the hearing of the wave.

After *In Memoriam* had been published, Tennyson stayed at Clevedon Court and made a pilgrimage to Hallam's tomb. "It seemed" he wrote, "a kind of consecration to go there".

The Great Hall

CLEVEDON

The town and resort of Clevedon owes much of its second flowering to Sir Arthur Halam Elton, who inherited the Court in 1853. A man of scholarship, he was also industrious, practical and generous in local affairs. Through his energetic leadership during some four decades, Clevedon became a beautiful and well-planned little town. In 1864 he introduced gaslight and the elegant wrought-iron pier (now, alas, but a relic) was locally financed, with Sir Arthur as chairman of the Pier Company, and opened in 1869.

The next baronet in this energetic and extremely versatile family was Sir Arthur's nephew Edmund (1846-1920) who combined the talents of inventor, mechanic and craftsman.

But it was his own handcraft achievements as a potter (with a local hunchback lad as assistant) that he became internationally known. The potter-baronet devised techniques incorporating colourful metallic glazes which attracted attention – and purchasers – on both sides of the Atlantic. A collection of Elton Ware is in the museum at the Court and Elton Ware mosaics and a large medallion decorate the clock tower in Clevedon, which Sir Edmund designed in celebration of Queen Victoria's Jubilee. He was succeeded by his son Ambrose the ninth baronet and a man of local affairs, upon whose death in 1951 his son, Sir Arthur Hallam Rice Elton became the tenth baronet; his talents led him to become a pioneer (with John Grierson) in the art and technology of documentary film-making. His historic house, with its splendid furnishings and intriguing Elton family pictures, is now itself a family 'documentary' for all to see, being in the care of the National Trust.

CLEVEDON

There was a very practical reason for the hill-top siting of Clevedon Old Church, whose roll of incumbents dates from 1331. The terrain towards the Court on the landward side, which is now well-drained pasture, was often under water. The lusty Severn tides swept over the flatlands from the village of Clevedon. In 1607 there was a particularly disastrous inundation.

The church was founded by the Augustinians who had settled at Bristol, where they started building the cathedral in 1142.

When Sir Charles Elton restored the Old Church in 1844 he renounced all rights to the manorial chapel of the lords of Clevedon in the south transept and handed it over to the parish. On the walls are a brass to members of the Elton family from 1742 to 1819 and memorial tablets to Eltons and their Hallam relations.

In a vault at the south end of the chapel lies Arthur Hallam.

A Norfolk girl whose name was to become known throughout the world was one of the candidates for confirmation who knelt before the Bishop of Bath and Wells in the church: Edith Louise Cavell (1865-1915), the patriot-nurse whose statue stands near Trafalgar Square, inscribed with her last words: "Patriotism is not enough. I must have no hatred or bitterness towards any one".

In charge of a Red Cross hospital at Brussels in 1914, Edith Cavell successfully assisted Allied soldiers to escape from Belgium. Her activities were discovered – she admitted them at her subsequent trial by court-martial – and she was shot at dawn on 11 October, 1915.

The old church

CREWKERNE

In the vale of a wide amphitheatre of hills, with the infant river Parrett ambling northwards towards Bridgwater, Crewkerne nudges the Dorset border. It is at least as old as King Alfred's time, for its name is an amalgam of Saxon and Celtic.

The prosperity of this little town and the villages around was founded on the weaving of serges; the Napoleonic Wars and the flax-growing in the district made it famous, transforming it into something of a boom-town with a vast output of sailcloth to satisfy maritime demands, both mercantile and naval.

When Nelson led his fleet into battle at Trafalgar, the canvasses of his *Victory* were made by Crewkerne sailmakers.

Sailcloth is still made there, though not of flax or cotton: it is almost exclusively the product of man-made fibres. The high quality is obviously maintained, for it was Crewkerne sailcloth which took Sir Francis Chichester on his world voyage, and several American and British competitors race under it for the America's Cup.

Nevertheless, the historic, stout natural canvas is still produced in the form of webbing for girths and many other uses, including seating for garden chairs.

East Coker, a nearby village once renowned for its "Coker Cloth" as well as for the making of sailcloth, has a place in both Puritan and literary history. It is the place whence T. S. Eliot's forbears migrated to "New England".

And the heart of the great, and devout, Anglo-American 20th-century writer and poet, lies buried in the church.

DODINGTON HOUSE

"Dodington House and St. Mary's Church, Restaurant, Bar and Exhibition Area". That is the leading index on the plan of the estate, embodied in the plushy illustrated brochure about the exquisite home of the Codrington family, situated ten miles north of Bath on the A26 road. Other indices refer to the sites of such attractions as the carriage museum, the display of crafts and the "Children's Adventureland and Diversities" as well as lakeside and woodland "trails".

The entire estate provides a prime example of the necessary adaptation of the past to ensure survival in the present, to the benefit of owner and public alike. The Codringtons and their youthful family still live in the magnificent rooms open to the public – except during the summer opening season, when they migrate to other quarters in the mansion.

The family's history is notable. A John Codrington, when 50, fought for Henry V at Agincourt in 1415 – and survived to the age of 111! In the 16th-century Giles Codrington, of neighbouring Didmarton, bought the Dodington estate. Another John was among the first settlers in Virginia in 1607. The Civil War led to the sequestration of the estate, later restored; but well before, in 1628, Christopher went off to the West Indies, where he made a large fortune in plantations and property deals. By the early 18th-century another Christopher bequeathed part of his West Indies property to found the Society for the Propagation of the Gospel, to which Codrington College, in Georgetown, Barbados, bears witness.

The Dodington estate eventually passed to Sir Christopher Bethell Codrington (1764-1839) and that is where the story of the present Dodington House begins.

DODINGTON HOUSE

Bethell Codrington started with two great advantages: he was very rich; and the park had already been landscaped by the famous Lancelot ('Capability') Brown. In the words of Alexander Pope: "the situation romantic, covered with woody hills stumbling upon one another confusedly, and the garden makes a valley betwixt them with some mounts and waterfalls".

The house took twenty years a-building, for Bethell was a perfectionist. He selected James Wyatt (1746-1813) as his architect. It is curious but fortunate that Wyatt, so closely associated with the Gothic Revival in architecture, should have designed the house in the lovely classical style of the Georgian period.

Adjoining the house, Wyatt built the church, its dome and Tuscan portico blending into the scene as a whole. It was there that Queen Mary sometimes worshipped when she was an "evacuee", living at the Duke of Beaufort's, at neighbouring Badminton, during the 1939-45 war.

There is a reminder of the war of 1914-18 – a window from Belgium. It was rescued by a Codrington from the ruins of the cathedral in the heavily bombarded town of Ypres.

The interior of the house combines grandeur with elegance. The spacious hall and double-staircase provide the grand manner *in excelsis,* and the reception rooms are elegance personified, and have known as guests such celebrities as William Pitt, the Prime Minister; Spencer Perceval, the Prime Minister who was assassinated in the House of Commons; and the first Duke of Wellington.

DODINGTON HOUSE

Masters of Dodington served their country with distinction on sea and land between the era of Nelson and the Crimea war in Victoria's reign. As First Lieutenant in HMS *Queen Charlotte,* Edward Codrington fought under Lord Howe's command in that Admiral's defeat of the French fleet in the three-day battle off Finisterre in 1794, culminating in 'The Glorious First of June'. Eleven years later, as a captain, he commanded HMS *Orion* at Trafalgar.

As a Vice-Admiral, Sir Christopher Codrington, then a KCB, was Commander-in-Chief at the battle of Navarino in 1827, defeating the Turkish fleet – and becoming a GCB. He was subsequently promoted to full Admiral. Sir Christopher sat as a Liberal M.P. for Devonport in 1832, 1835 and 1837, but resigned his seat on his appointment, in 1839, as Commander-in-Chief, Portsmouth.

During the Crimea war another member of the family made his mark. General Sir William Codrington, GCB, commanded the First Brigade, Light Division, at the battle of the Alma.

In 1876 a baronetcy was conferred upon Gerald Codrington. The present baronet's son, Major Simon Codrington is the owner of Dodington.

In his welcome to visitors he writes (with a touch of charming understatement) of the domestic aspect of present-day life: "Although the rooms are a little larger than in most houses and everything looks rather grand, Dodington is our home and, believe me, my wife has exactly the same problems running a house as everyone else does, often considerably magnified".

DUNSTER

When, in 1976, Lieut.-Colonel Walter Lutterell presented his hill-top castle at Dunster to the National Trust to hold in perpetuity (one fervently hopes) for the public to relish and enjoy, he made a gift of surpassing beauty with a background rich in the history of more than 1,000 years. It stands high over a setting so pictorially lovely as to be almost unbelievably romantic – a fairy-tale spot, yet only a few hundred yards from the busy main road (A396) east of Minehead.

On the site once stood a Saxon fortress. When the Normans came the Conqueror granted it to the de Mohuns, but the oldest existing masonry is the late 13th-century gateway. By 1376 the Castle had changed hands. Elizabeth Lutterell bought the demesne from the de Mohuns, and it remained in the family until Colonel Lutterell gave it to the National Trust – after exactly six centuries of occupation by his family.

It is relevant to mention that Dunster was not the Lutterells' oldest home in this delectable district. Court House, a few miles away at East Quantoxhead (referred to on another page) has remained in the family since 1230, and in the hands of their Paganel ancestors before them, from the time of the Conquest.

By the early 17th-century there were many alterations and additions to Dunster Castle which made it somewhat less austere as a habitation. Much of the modernisation was the work of William Arnold, who was responsible for Wadham College, Oxford. But its present appearance was given to the Castle in Victorian times by the celebrated architect-restorer Anthony Salvin.

DUNSTER

The Castle contains some exceptional treasures and its pictures and furnishings some fascinating historical reminders of the Civil War. The Lutterells were staunch royalists. The Prince of Wales (later Charles II) stayed there when his father sent him to enlist westcountry support for the royalist cause. Later, the Castle was besieged by the Roundheads and after holding out for 160 days the garrison was forced to surrender in 1646.

Ironically, the wealth of portraits include one of Oliver Cromwell.

In the banqueting hall, above the dramatically-carved staircase, are the six renowned leather wall-hangings, brightly coloured, telling the love-story of Antony and Cleopatra.

The Lutterells have been fortunate in their women-folk. We have seen how Elizabeth's activities in real estate obtained the Castle from the de Mohuns in 1376 – she paid 5,000 marks for it – and among the portraits is one of Dame Margaret, painted in 1562 when she was 62 years of age. The National Trust's excellent guidebook tells us that after the death of her husband, Sir Andrew Lutterell, Dame Margaret "made a great success of managing the family estates which passed in turn to her two elder sons, both of whom she outlived".

Allegory abounds in what is certainly the Castle's most dramatic picture. Dated 1550, it depicts shipwrecked Sir John Lutterell. He is bare to the waist and triton-like below water level, raising an arm to be caressed and calmed by a naked women bearing an olive branch, representing Peace, while to her left a semi-nude Venus calms the horse of War.

DUNSTER

Coastwise from the Castle is Conygar Hill. It is topped by a so-called lookout tower, designed in 1776 at a cost of £192. In fact it is just one of those "follies", so popular in the 18th-century, the work of a landscape artist. But it is a compelling landmark of Dunster from the main road.

The High Street, at the base of the Castle's hill, is a happy jumble of buildings of various periods – many of them shops and cafes for tourists – but the cynosure is certainly the free-standing Yarn Market.

This charming building is octagonal, gabled, fenestrated, colonnaded at its base and crowned by a little octagonal, gabled cupola. It was built by George Lutterell in 1609, but had to be repaired in 1647, after the Civil War had brought the Roundheads to besiege the Castle.

The Yarn Market has erected to serve a vital commercial purpose. From the fleece of Exmoor sheep, Dunster folk produced yarn for the cloth known as "Dunsters" – and named as such in an Act in the reign of James I. Merchants came to buy this commodity for the manufacture of "kersey-meres". Doubtless they then repaired for refreshment to the Ship Inn, a few yards away.

The house was originally built for the Abbot of Cleeve, but was bought by the Lutterells in 1499. Today, the Ship Inn is the Lutterell Arms Hotel; but in the heyday of the Yarn Market its original name was appropriate enough, because a mile or so from the village was Dunster's little harbour – but the sea receded and the harbour silted up.

The Old Yarn Market

Priory Church

DUNSTER

There is more, much more, of historic and architectural interest in Dunster than the two focal points of the Castle and the Yarn Market.

The Priory Church of St. George, of red sandstone and with a massive square tower, buttressed and embattled, contains an unique feature: its rood screen, with fourteen openings and supporting a gallery, is the longest in England. The tower, started in 1443 and finished three years later, houses a noteworthy clock. It chimes every four hours, day and night; it provides a different tune for every day of the week; and at Christmas it plays the celebrated 'Dunster Carol' among its repertoire of carols.

In Church Street, standing among dwellings of attractive character but of much later periods, is a very long, slate-hung 14th-century house, The Nunnery. It is a misnomer, for there is no evidence of it ever having been inhabited by nuns. It was, however, originally monastic property, for it was the guest-house of Dunster's Benedictine Priory, annexed as a cell to Bath Abbey, which is now in the new County of Avon.

Eggs and young table-birds ("squabs" as unfledged pigeons are still known in rural places) were provided for the Priory's brethren from its dovecote, which happily remains in a fine state of preservation, tucked away in what was the Priory's ancillary land, now a garden. The cote is a huge round building of stone. Inside, the revolving ladder providing human access is still in working order.

DYRHAM PARK

William Blathwayt, who died in 1717, was a highly efficient and successful man. In the course of his diplomatic and political career he was engaged in public business at The Hague, Rome and Stockholm; secretary-at-war; clerk to the privy council. From 1692 until 1710 he held the secretaryship of state.

But it was two years before the accession of William and Mary that Blathwayt brought off a domestic *coup* which was to associate Dyrham Park with his name for generations to come: he married Miss Mary Wynter, the 36-years-old heiress to Dryham. The marriage was short, for Mary died after five years, although not before she had become a mother four times.

Blathwayt, now a rich man, set about rebuilding Dyrham, then a decaying Tudor manor-house, to transform it into a palatial mansion.

The lovely south Cotswold parkland site, a few miles north of Bath off the A46 road and with Bristol to its west, was first mentioned in the Saxon Chronicle of the year 891. If, as is thought, the name derives from the phonetically similar Saxon *deor-hamm,* signifying deer enclosure, it is among the oldest recorded deer parks in England.

During the war of 1939-45 part of the house was used as a hospital. The house and contents, also the gardens, were acquired by the nation in 1956 and are now in the care of the National Trust.

The splendid deer park is also secure. Mr. J. R. W. Blathwayt generously gave covenants over the land to protect it from development.

SOUTH GLAMORGAN
MOUTH OF THE SE
WESTON SUPER MARE
BRIDGWATER BAY
BRENDON
PORLOCK
MINEHEAD
DUNSTERD
WATCHET
ST. AUDRIES
EAST QUANTOXHEAD
KILVE
HOLFORD
NETHER STOW
CLEEVE ABBEY
WILLITON
EXMOOR
BRENDON HILLS
Tarr Steps
BRIDGEW
SOMERSET
TAUNTON
WELLINGTON
BAMPTON
DEVON

THORNBURY
AUST
CHIPPING SODBURY
BADMINGTON HOUSE
DODINGTON
CHIPPENHAM
BRISTOL
NAILSEA
KELSTON
BATHFORD
BATHAMPTON
CLAVERTON
BATH
AVON
NORTON ST. PHILIP
WILTSHIRE
BURRINGTON
MENDIP HILLS
CHEWTON MENDIP
CHEDDAR
WESTBURY
MELLS
FROME
WOOKEY HOLE
NUNNEY CASTLE
WELLS
SHEPTON MALLET
GLASTONBURY
ANSFORD
SEDGEMOOR 1685
CASTLE CARY
SOMERTON
LYTES CARY
ILCHESTER
MONTACUTE HOUSE
YEOVIL
SHERBORNE
CREWKERNE
DORSET
Nicola Luscombe 11.4.78.

DRYHAM PARK

The first William Balthwayt was not only financially fortunate in marrying an heiress, he was also culturally lucky in having an uncle in Thomas Povey, a man of cultured taste whose guidance, from his nephew's early age, gave him the ability to appreciate beautiful things. But Povey was no business man, according to the precise Samuel Pepys who succeeded him as treasurer to the Commission for Tangier. The diarist wrote scathingly of him as "the simple Povey, of all the most ridiculous fools that I ever saw to attend to business".

Nevertheless, Pepys was quite fulsome in his admiration for the fine taste displayed in the contents of Povey's London house. Among the praises which he lavished on them were Povey's "delicate pictures, and above all, a piece of perspective in his closet".

That "perspective" may be described as a *trompe-l'oeil:* it depicts a long tiled corridor with a mop and a dog in the foreground and an offended cat in the middle distance. It now hangs at Dyrham. In 1693 Uncle Povey sold ninety-three pictures and some five hundred books to William Blathwayt – for £500.

A splendid reminder of the pre-Blathwayt era in the adjoining church is the richly sculptured tomb of the 16th-century George Wynter (a forebear of Mary, who became Blathwayt's wife) with his figure, his wife's and their eleven children. One of their four boys circumnavigated the world in Sir Francis Drake's expedition.

Also in the church are no fewer than nine escutcheons, commemmorating the Blathwayts and their wives from 1717 until 1871.

Balcony room

EAST QUANTOXHEAD

An air of timelessness pervades this tiny *cul-de-sac* village between the main road and the Bristol Channel. Not surprisingly, perhaps, since it has been the home of one family, the Lutterells, (as mentioned under the heading of Dunster) for some seven-and-a-half centuries. Unlike Dunster Castle, the E-shaped Court House of grey stone is a private dwelling and not open to the public.

It stands secluded but very close to the village pond, Court Farm and a cluster of thatched cottages: a setting of utter tranquility on the seaward edge of the Quantock Hills. Its little church, rich in wood carvings on pulpit and bench-ends, contains the 16th-century tomb of Sir Hugh Lutterell beneath a sculptured canopy.

The tranquil seclusion of East Quantoxhead, however, burst into national notoriety in the 18th-century. It became the birthplace of Sarah Biffen, the daughter of humble cottagers, in 1784. She was born legless and armless, yet became celebrated as an artist.

Her parents sold her to a fairground impresario, who exhibited her as a freak: she even appeared as such at London's age-old Bartholomew Fair. Later, she overcame her terrible physical handicap and showed her artistic ability. With a brush affixed to her shoulder she developed into a talented portraitist after a titled patron had paid for her art lessons.

Fame came, and even royalty patronised her work. In 1821, at the age of 37, she won the Society of Arts medal. Sad to say, Sarah fell into poverty in her later years, but that bluff sailor-monarch William IV granted her a pension.

FROME

Folk settled here in Saxon times and St. Aldhelm, the energetic and literary priest who became successively Abbot of Malmesbury and Bishop of Sherborne and died in 709, established at Frome a stone church. Nothing now remains but it was probably akin to the still existing Saxon church of St. Lawrence at Bradford-on-Avon. Aldhelm's church was still standing in the 12th-century. In 934 King Athelstan, the favourite grandson of Alfred the Great, held a Witanagemot at Frome, and it was there that Dunstan's successor, King Edred, died in 955.

At the Norman Conquest, Frome had already begun to emerge as a place of some note, the head of a "Hundred" and having its own market. King William bestowed the church lands on his Chancellor, upon whose death they were given to the Abbey of Cirencester, which held them until the Dissolution. Meanwhile through the centuries the lordship of the manor passed by descent until sold to the Earl of Cork and Orrery, head of the Boyle family, in the mid-18th-century; though the erstwhile monastic lands in the town and neighbouring manors and parts of the nearby ancient royal forest of Selwood, were acquired by the family of Thynne.

The Thynnes' ancestral home, Longleat, is but a few miles away on the Wiltshire border. The family's present head, the sixth Marquess of Bath, has made it known to countless thousands as a "stately home" combined with a lion park and other attractions.

The town of Frome, however, has attractions of a different kind.

Parish Church

FROME

The town sensibly lay fairly low in the Civil War although the townsfolk, unlike some of the neighbouring gentry, favoured the Parliament to the extent that church bells rang out to celebrate a Roundhead victory, but remained silent for a Royalist one. The people were equable and industrious and more interested in earning prosperity, notably through weaving, than in taking part in fratricidal affairs of State.

The same attitude of non-intervention was made manifest during the Monmouth Rebellion of 1685. After a skirmish at Norton St. Philip (which nearly cost him his life) the Duke withdrew to Frome, hoping to whip up some support. But the townspeople did little more than politely tolerate his presence during the couple of days he spent among them and, minus some deserters, he moved his pathetic little force off towards Bridgwater, to meet final defeat at Sedgemoor while the people of Frome quietly got on with their commercial activities of cloth-making and dyeing.

Even so, when the terrible Judge Jeffreys came to Somerset, he found a dozen men in Frome to be hanged.

The compassionate Thomas Ken, then Bishop of Bath and Wells, pulled all the strings he could to intercede for the simple Somerset folk arraigned at Jeffreys' Bloody Assize – but in vain.

He lies buried at Frome, in the parish church. After being deprived of his See, he spent his time at Longleat. When he died in 1717, his request that he be buried in his former diocese was observed. Frome was the nearest spot on Somerset soil and within his old diocese of Bath and Wells.

FROME

The town grew apace in the 18th- and early 19th-century, diversifying its industries to make up for the decline in cloth-working due to more competitive modern methods in the north of England, and by 1881 there were no fewer than 90 firms, large and small. And adaptation to industrial demands of today is still a feature of the town. Yet it retains both a medieval and a Georgian charm; on its hillsides are some lovely little streets and passageways, and engaging placenames like Gentle Street, Saxon Vale, Vernal Lane, Packsaddle Way and Kissing Batch.

Although it managed to side-step the Civil War and the Monmouth Rebellion it experienced a major political rough-and-tumble in 1832: a riot at the George and the Crown inns at the parliamentary election of 1832. Of the opposing candidates, mill-owner Thomas Sheppard and landowner Sir Thomas Champneys, there is no doubt that Champneys was the aggressor. He came to the hustings with about 500 toughs, some mounted, armed with cudgels and other weapons. Sheppard's small band of well-behaved supporters were unarmed. Rioting continued for four days and immense damage to persons and property was done, one injury proving fatal.

The Magistrates swore-in Special Constables and armed some of them with carbines. They ejected the rioters from the George and barricaded the building.

At last, after Dragoons visited the town on two of the days, matters calmed down enough for polling to take place. Happily, intimidation and violence did not pay. The peaceable Sheppard was returned with a majority of 63 out of the total of 263 votes cast.

Blue House

FROME

Frome is a hilly town, leading down to the level plain and to the bridge over the river which bears its name, near the spot where St. Aldhelm built his mission-station more than thirteen hundred years ago.

Adjoining the bridge, on land once bedevilled with the flooding of the river, stands the Blue House, a triumph of restoration and adaptation. It has been listed in the top grade of 'Scheduled Buildings' and largely thanks to the public-spiritedness of all sections of the community in raising funds, "their" Blue House has been re-born.

William Loversedge, the lord of the manor, founded an almshouse there in the 15th-century. It was replaced by another which had become so dilapidated by the 18th-century that it was demolished and a bigger building took its place – but this time to combine an almshouse for old women with a charity school. The townsfolk subscribed to its foundation and individual benefactors provided endowments. The schoolboys wore a blue uniform – therefore it was called The Blue School.

Its dual purpose was symbolised by the stature of an old woman, "Nancy Guy", in a niche on the facade and below her, on the broken pediment of the main door, that of a schoolboy, "Billy Ball".

In the present century it ceased to be a school but remains an almshouse, where since its recent restoration there is provision for eighteen flats equipped with every modern amenity.

GLASTONBURY

An incomparable mystique pervades Glastonbury and its countryside, where history blends with legend. Its origins are as clouded as the mists which at times enshroud the flat pastures towards the Bristol Channel at Bridgwater Bay.

The marshland, long since irrigated, includes several small hills – "islands" – and Glastonbury's site is the Isle of Avalon, from the name given to it by the Romans: Insula Avalonia. The substantial and exquisite remains of its Abbey stand on one of the most sacred Christian spots in Britain.

The Glastonbury legend is that in A.D. 60 Philip the Apostle sent Joseph of Armathea to preach the gospel in Britain. At Glastonbury he thrust his staff into the ground and it took root, flowered as a thorn tree and has since always blossomed twice a year – in spring and at Christmas-time. A Holy Thorn is still to be seen in the Abbey grounds.

Also within the Abbey ruins is a spot marking the site of the remains of the semi-legendary King Arthur, and of his Queen, Guinevere. The story of Arthur, an amorphous figure for centuries, was given a poetic boost when Caxton printed Sir Thomas Malory's *Morte d'Arthur* in 1485, and a strong refresher in the age of Victorian romanticism through Tennyson, with his *Idylls of the King.* Then came the composer Rutland Boughton (founder of the Glastonbury Festival Players in 1914) who wrote *The Round Table* and other highly successful musical dramas based on the Arthurian legends.

In 1965 amid the Abbey ruins a tall, plain Cross was erected to mark the ancient Christian place, the origin of which is known only in legend. It is oaken, and came from the Duchy of Cornwall estate: a gift from Queen Elizabeth II.

Abbey Ruins

GLASTONBURY

Glastonbury's most significant native was undoubtedly St. Dunstan, its Abbot in the middle of the 10th-century and Archbishop of Canterbury for twenty-seven years up to his death in 988. He was the first example of an English statesman who was not a warrior, and combined saintliness with great administrative gifts. During his abbacy Glastonbury became a centre of learning and he erected monastic buildings ancillary to the church.

Dunstan did much to advance secular civilisation and he was fearless in purifying religious teaching and practice, drawing up codes for the enforcement of ecclesiastical discipline. In the period of his archiepiscopacy he was the most powerful subject in the kingdom and his statesmanship contributed vitally to the successful reign of his king, Edgar the Peaceable.

By the time of the Conquest Glastonbury was already wealthy. Normans began to re-build the abbey but in 1184 fire almost completely destroyed it, and its records. The earliest remains now standing majestically, surrounded by lawns and engirdled with trees, are those of the re-built abbey, dating from the early 13th-century.

The Abbots became great (and often ostentatious) magnates in medieval times, for the abbacy on the isolated Isle of Avalon controlled rich estates and exercised considerable power, both temporal and spiritual. The Abbey itself was vast – longer than Wells Cathedral by 200 feet.

The regal splendour and wealth of the Abbots who "ruled" over huge portions of Wessex fostered the snide and penetrating – and amusingly irreverent – comment that "if the Abbot of Glastonbury were to marry the Abbess of Shaftesbury, their first-born would own more land than the King of England".

Abbot's Kitchen

GLASTONBURY

Dominating Glastonbury and the Vale of Avalon is the steep, conical hill which is Somerset's most respected landmark: Glastonbury Tor. It was the scene of high tragedy on a November day in 1539, when the last Abbot met his unmerited and grisly death.

Cardinal Wolsey had nominated Richard Whiting, who was appointed Abbot in 1525. It was a good choice, for Whiting – a member of an old and landed west-country family – was a sound administrator and a cultivated man of peace. But when Henry VIII dissolved the monasteries and Thomas Cromwell had succeeded the disgraced Wolsey and had become the King's chief minister (promising to make his master the richest monarch in Christendom), the hapless Whiting was conveniently accused of treason.

His death was inevitable, because *before* he was brought to trial the ruthless Cromwell had issued a written instruction that "the Abbot of Glaston to be tried at Glaston and also executed there".

In the event, the grisly charade of a 'trial' took place at Wells. Thence the old Abbot was taken to Glastonbury, lashed to a hurdle and dragged by a horse to the summit of the Tor, and hanged.

The wooden chair in which Richard Whiting sat at his trial is on view in the Bishop's Palace at Wells. It is a permanent memorial to him, for its design, known as the Glastonbury Chair, is still reproduced and is among the chancel furniture of many of our parish churches.

The Tor

GLASTONBURY

After the Dissolution the fabric of the great Benedictine Abbey suffered the fate of most other monastic properties. The 'locals' purloined timber, lead and stone as materials for lay building. Yet both inside the grounds and in the town itself are substantial remains to be seen today, notably the huge, freestanding 14th-century abbot's kitchen; the imposing barn for storing grain; and a sizeable stone building which served the dual purpose of a fish store and a dwelling for the fishermen whose job was to keep the monks supplied with permitted food for Lent and the many other days of fasting.

In the High Street is an early 16th-century building which was the law court where the abbots, in their landowning capacity exercised jurisdiction over the laity.

Glastonbury naturally attracted pilgrims, as it now attracts tourists. Henry VII paid a visit in 1494, possibly not so much for purely pious reasons as to display a show of majesty in the westcountry, for he was at that period saddled with the problem of coping with the imposter Perkin Warbeck's claim to the throne. Pilgrims provided a rich source of revenue for the Abbey.

He was lodged in the Abbot's house, where visitors of high rank (and ample means) were accommodated. But other wealthy pilgrims of less exalted status stayed in a splendid hostlery in High Street: the George, which was known up to the earlier part of this century as the George and Pilgrim.

Stone-faced, three-storied, battlemented and admirably maintained within, the George was built by an Abbot in the 15th-century. It is one of the very few pre-Reformation inns in England.

Abbot's house

Alfoxton Park

HOLFORD

William Wordsworth was the most celebrated resident of Holford, but not the most popular one. The man who was to become Poet Laureate in 1843 leased Alfoxton Park in 1797 and his known sympathies with the objects of the French Revolution (albeit, like most egalitarian intellectuals before and since, they were confined to theory, not practice) led to grave suspicion among gentry and cottagers alike, that he was up to no good. Why, for example, did this terrifying Radical young poet take such long walks *at night?*

The Government even sent an agent – an MI5 man in today's language – to keep an eye on him and other potential spies in the area. And when his year's lease expired the St Aubyn family, then the owners, refused to renew the tenancy!

Wordsworth, then 27, lived at Alfoxton with his sister Dorothy. The annual rent of that delectable house, set in a deer-park with magnificent views of the sloping countryside to the sea and the Welsh coast beyond, was £23. In the early 1920s, when it became my family home for several years, the rent was £400. Even so, it was a "snip", for the estate totalled 180 sporting acres, including woodland and the wild and lovely Holford Glen – and even by then a bathroom in the house though, like the Wordsworths, we depended on candles and oil lamps for lighting.

Alfoxton Park has passed through several hands since then. It is now an excellent country-house hotel, retaining most of the glamour of the past yet none of the rural inconveniences of such things as a temperamental water supply and oil lamps.

Holford Glen

HOLFORD

Alfoxton Park is a mile or so from the village, which starts at the Plough inn, on a corner of the main road from Bridgwater to Minehead, and is the debouching point of some beautiful Quantock combes.

At the entrance to the long drive, bordered by a wood and the Glen, is the Dogpound. This relic is a square stone structure with a slit at the eye-level of a mounted man so that he could see and reclaim any of his dogs impounded there. In Wordsworth's time foxhounds were kennelled at the top of the Park. The spot is separated from the Dogpound by a flat measure of arable land known anciently as a "hide" and is mentioned in the Domesday Survey. (The field is still known as "cross hides"). Thence a sharp, woody declivity leads to the Dogpound, which owes its existence to a tragedy, recounted by Wordsworth in a poem.

Meat for the hounds was hung upon nearby trees, and those "larders" attracted prowling dogs, leaping and snarling for pieces. The uproar would start the hounds a-baying and one night when the huntsman turned out of his cottage to silence them he forgot to don his huntsman's coat. Without that familiar sight – and scent – the hounds did not recognise him and tore him to pieces. Thereafter, The Dogpound was built for the incarceration of non-hounds.

Alongside the Dogpound is a rough, steep track which was once a road for wheeled vehicles bound for Staple, West Quantoxhead (St. Audries), Bicknoller and other north Quantock villages. On the crest it passed the superb line of Holford Beeches. The magnificent trees mark the topmost boundary of Alfoxton Park.

Combe House

HOLFORD

This quiet, sequestered village has had an industrial history. It has known a silk factory and a tannery; in the nearby hamlet of Dodington there was even a copper mine.

Some Huguenot exiles settled at Holford in the early 16-century and established a silk factory at the head of Holford Glen, in the village's centre. Its ruins may still be seen by peering through the undergrowth beneath what is still known as "factory wall". Power came from several water-wheels operated by the tumbling stream in the Glen and the soft Quantock water was excellent for dyeing. When the Revolution put an end to the import of raw silk from France the factory switched to blanket-making until 1820, when a disastrous fire closed it.

The Hayman family of Combe House, in Tannery Combe and now an hotel, has for generations played a leading part in the life and fortunes of Holford. In the early 19th-century James Hayman built a tannery: the 1893 successor to his original water-wheel can still be seen, adjoining Combe House. For tanning he not only used the raw material from the oaks in the combe, but even imported Valonia oak-bark from Asia Minor. Eventually the tanyard fell into disuse, though in 1886 it was resuscitated by his nephew, John James Hayman. But it was not to last long, for by 1900 Continental competition forced its closure.

But J. J. Hayman was indefatigable. In the same year he kept his wheel turning for the private production of electric light; for power for a stone-cracking machine; for a chaff-cutter; and even for a machine for cleaning boots.

HOLFORD

Village churches often have complicated and elusive histories, and so it is with Holford's, but in his excellent booklet *A Brief History of Holford,* published in 1973 and obtainable locally, my old acquaintance Mr. Atkin Hayman tells us that the names of incumbents are known from 1272 to the present day. By 1832 the building was virtually in ruins but an energetic rector saw it re-built – probably largely at his own expense – and the job was finished by 1842.

So typical of the Victorian era, the Saxon stone font was discarded as "unsuitable" and was replaced by one of marble.

More than threescore years later a succeeding rector campaigned for the very reasonable ambition of giving the church a pulpit. Mr J. J. Hayman (mentioned on the previous page) gave some seasoned oak for the purpose. Then the rector discovered, entombed in the rectory cellar, the Saxon font. It is now back again in the church, though not for baptisms: the ancient relic forms the base of the pulpit made from Hayman's oaken gift.

Since then, much more has been added to that little church (which was probably built astride a pre-Christian trackway) notably an attractive lych-gate. Strangers who pass through it may like to know that Wordsworth was not the only national celebrity associated with Holford, for in the church-yard lies Frederick Norton.

His famous musical extravaganza *Chu-Chin-Chow,* which from 1916 had a London run of 2,238 consecutive performances, is still being performed in many parts of the world.

Old Cottages

ILCHESTER

The Romans called it Londinis and it was an important military base, being on the road junction from Bath to the north, Weymouth Bay to the south and Exeter to the south-west, thence skirting Dartmoor at North Tawton and on to Cornwall.

Ilchester has seen stirring events, both dynastic and domestic, down the centuries but there are few visible remains of them. It was once the county town of Somerset, possessing the country's only polling station and its only jail which, owing to the insufferable conditions therein, earned the town the unenviable nickname of "Jailchester".

This now quiet little town can drop a couple of celebrated names among its list of natives. In the early 13th-century that famous Franciscan monk and scientist, Roger Bacon, was born and educated there. In his later studies of nature, alchemy and optics he is credited with having discovered an explosive compound of charcoal, saltpetre and sulphur – the forerunner of gunpowder.

Another native, some 450 years after Bacon, was Elizabeth Singer, who became in 1710 Mrs Elizabeth Rowe, the popular authoress and poet whose work earned praise from Dr. Samuel Johnson – and even secured her a place in the Dictionary of National Biography.

The town once had a famous playwright as its M.P.: Richard Brinsley Sheridan.

For the special Ilchester cheese, now appreciated nationwide among the discriminating, we have to thank a landlord of the elegant old Ivelchester Hotel, an inn of coaching days in the town's centre. To the "mix" for locally-made Cheddar cheese he added a compound of herbs and – beer!

Ivelchester Hotel

ILMINSTER

Two days before Christmas in 1819 an unusual equipage arrived at the George Inn at Ilminster. The travellers were the Duke of Kent and his formidable German wife with their child. His impecunious Royal Highness, the youngest of George III's litter of four sons, was probably *en route* for the coast to spend an economical Christmas in the mild climate of east Devon.

The child was precisely seven months old. It was the first hotel she had ever stayed at, as a plaque on the front records. She was to become fatherless two years later but his infant daughter Victoria was to ascend the throne eighteen years after the visit to Ilminster, and to become Empress of India before the close of her long, historic reign.

The present minster church – the first syllable of the town's name refers to its river, the Isle – dates from about 1450, though Ilminster's roll of vicars starts in the reign of Edward the Confessor. It is among the foremost of Somerset's beautiful towered and pinnacled churches.

In the north transept is the tomb of Sir William Wadham, who died in 1452. His grandson, Nicholas, bequeathed to his widow the responsibility of founding Wadham College, Oxford, which was completed in 1613 and was to number among its alumni Robert Blake and Christopher Wren. Opposite Wadham's, in the south transept, is the tomb of Humphrey Walrond, who founded the Grammar School nearly 500 years ago. Today, his school is no more. There is a 20th-century Comprehensive in the town, and after the age of 13, boys and girls have to travel to Crewkerne.

Dillington House

ILMINSTER

Although Ilminster's ancient Grammar School no longer exists, its educational tradition has been happily brought into modern times by the Somerset County Council by the skilful adaptation of the stately Dillington House as an adult education and arts centre. Local folk as well as individuals, societies and other groups from afar, come for cultural refreshment in this splendidly equipped old house in a lovely rural setting near the town. Upwards of 30,000 people attend each year an almost bewildering range of courses, both residential and day, from music, art and drama to more esoteric subjects.

One feels that if Humphrey Walrond could arise from his pedimented tomb in the Lady-Chapel of the Minster Church he would be (almost) fully consoled for the extinction of his Grammar School by the realisation that senior education – albeit in a form unknown in his time – was flourishing on the fringe of Ilminster.

The 16th-century house was once owned by the Speke family, one of whose 19th-century descendants was the explorer John Hanning Speke, discoverer of the source of the Nile at Lake Victoria Nyanza. Through marriage with a Speke, Dillington came into the possession of the hapless Lord North, Prime Minister to George III. Although opposed to war with the American colonists he was influenced by his royal master against his own judgment – yet remained in office for six years after the Declaration of Independence in 1776.

But at Dillington he could enjoy a quiet country retreat, although even in Somerset he was involved in public life to some extent: he was the county's Lord-Lieutenant.

Kelston Park

KELSTON

Etheldreda was a bastard daughter of Henry VIII, who gave her the manor of Kelston, which had belonged to the Abbey of Shaftesbury until the Dissolution. The king's treasurer for camps and buildings, a powerful job under a monarch who was such a great builder of defensive works along the south coast, was John Harington. In 1546 he became master of the manor – some three miles west of Bath – by becoming Etheldreda's husband. Their son, Sir John Harington (1561-1612) was a godson of Princess Elizabeth, Henry's daughter by Anne Boleyn.

He entertained his godmother at Kelston in 1592 when, as Queen, she visited Bath – then a walled medieval town and apparently a more than usually smelly one, because on her departure from the salubrious air of Kelston she gave her godson £500 "to alleviate the stinks of Bath".

Sir John was a man of parts, a poet, satyrist and epigrammist with also a mechanical turn of mind, for he is credited with inventing the water-closet – though not yet complete with the refinement of the ball-valve for replenishing the cistern!

The present fine mansion and its spacious ancillary buildings stand well away from the village on a lovely site, its terrace overlooking the Avon valley. It was built in 1760 for Sir Caesar Hawkins – a magnate who doubtless did well from the flourishing Bristol slave-trade – to the design of John Wood the Younger, son of the initial creator of Georgian Bath. The estate later passed, through the Neelds, to the Inigo Jones family, by whom it was long occupied as a private residence. It is now a residential centre for the Methodist Association of Youth Clubs.

KILVE

Wordsworth called it "Kilve by the green sea": perhaps he was colour-blind. Green are the hills behind and verdant the lane to the sea through the straggling village which lies so comfortably off the main Bridgwater-Minehead main road, where stands the Hood Arms.

Near the church are the ruins of a priory, founded in 1329. Half-a-mile beyond, agricultural land extends to the very edge of the shore, over a gap for the outflow of the Quantock stream which has tumbled down through Holford Glen. It is an uncharitable foreshore, rocky and muddy, a study of greys and browns, and far from sea-green. But an ideal spot for a curious sport known as *glatting,* of which the idyllic Wordsworth would not have approved. At low tide in autumn huge and ferocious conger eels are prised from under the rocks by parties of villagers armed with wooden stakes and accompanied by a variety of dogs: a muddy and bloody business, but hilarious withal.

Kilve, however, is proud to claim a place in the history of sport through its rector, from 1910-1938: the Reverend D. Hartwell James, one of the dying breed of sporting parsons. A loveable, genial man, Parson James had a good and quick eye with a gun, but it was as a trout fisherman – wet fly – that he was nationally renowned. He told me that he never had to buy fishing equipment because manufacturers were proud to supply him gratis. But he did not hunt. In his pulpit, on Sundays before the opening meet of staghounds, he was wont to refer to the hymn "As pants the hart for cooling streams when wounded in the chase". Emotion caused him to weep and wipe away a tear with his surplice. I have seen him do so.

Hanging Chapel

LANGPORT

Almost all that remains of the defences of the ancient walled town of Langport is the "hanging chapel" built over its east gate in 1353. Down the hill towards the level of the river Parrett are some fine buildings which reflect Langport's 18th and 19th-century commercial heyday when it was literally a port: river navigation and trading enterprise made it a busy centre of two-way traffic in barge-hauled merchandise.

A leading merchant was the banker and shipowner Thomas Watson Bagehot (pronounced Ba-jot) to whom was born in 1827 a son, Walter, who was to become famous as an immensely influential writer on political, social and economic subjects.

Walter Bagehot studied at University College, London, and was called to the Bar in 1852, though in the same year he returned to Langport to enter his father's business. He soon became known as a writer of vigorous and lucid articles, also of literary criticism.

Of his books, the most lastingly significant is *The English Constitution*, published in 1867 and subsequently translated into French and German, as was his *Physics and Politics*, which appeared in 1872. He was also the author of *Lombard Street: A Description of the Money Market*.

When he was thirty-one he married. His bride was Eliza, daughter of James Wilson, founder and editor of *The Economist*. When his father-in-law died in 1860 he succeeded to the editorial chair.

He held the editorship until his death in 1877 at his birthplace, Langport.

LYTES CARY

Botany, genealogy and hymn-writing distinguished the Lyte family of Lytes Cary, near Ilchester, which they occupied from 1286 until the middle of the 18th-century.

In 1578 Henry Lyte made a horticultural mark by publishing *A niewe Herball or History of Plantes.* Although it was not an original work, having been translated from French, it was a runaway success, further editions being published in 1586, 1595 and 1619. It was still being reprinted in 1678. The author had seen to it that his book had the best of launchings, for he astutely dedicated it to Queen Elizabeth, datelined "from my poore house at Lytescarie".

As a genealogical author, Henry Lyte was equally brilliant in his promotional activities. He wrote a book, *The Light of Britaigne,* purporting to prove to his countrymen that they were descended from the Trojans. It was published in 1588, and with an exquisite sense of the publicity value of good timing, a copy was presented to the Queen on the very day that she went in state to St. Paul's to give thanks for the defeat of the Spanish Armada.

The Reverend Henry Francis Lyte (1793-1847) was the author of well-known hymns, including *Abide With Me*. But before his time the property had passed to other hands and had reached an advanced state of decay until rescued in 1907, when it came into the possession of Sir Walter Jenner, the second baronet and son of Queen Victoria's physician. He thoroughly restored Lytes Cary. He died in 1948, leaving the house and much of its contents to the National Trust.

MELLS

Old nursery rhymes are often political in origin and one of the best-known, *Little Jack Horner,* is said to refer to Mells, a lovely village between Frome and Leigh-on-Mendip. The story goes that John Horner, a local agent for the Abbot of Glastonbury, was deputed by him to take to Henry VIII a pie containing many of the great Abbey's property deeds in the vain hope of appeasing the King; but Horner was tempted to delve under the crust and purloin one of the title-deeds. The "plum" he pulled out was that of the title to Mells manor.

However that may be, the manor was in the possession of the Horners from the Dissolution until the earlier part of this century. The last of the male Horners, Sir John, was buried in the churchyard adjoining his manor-house in the late 1920s. The family were staunch Liberals. Sir John's daughter had married Raymond, son of the Liberal statesman H. H. Asquith (subsequently Earl of Oxford and Asquith) by his first marriage. In the war of 1914-18 both the last Horner of the male line and Raymond Asquith were killed in action and the manor passed to Mrs. Raymond Asquith.

In the Horner chapel of the splendid 16th-century church is a beautiful but unusual feature: an equestrian statue. The mounted figure is that of Raymond Asquith, in military uniform. The sculptor was Sir Alfred Munnings.

At the time of Sir John Horner's death the rector of Mells was an Irishman of great wit and charm and a distinguished theological writer – Canon James O. Hannay. But to a vast public in Britain and America he was known under his pen-name of George A. Birmingham, a best-selling writer of humourous fiction between 1908 and 1931.

Church Steps

MINEHEAD

The observant and peripatetic Daniel Defoe (1661-1731), who won an abiding place in journalism and authorship even if he had never written *Robinson Crusoe,* described Minehead as "the best port and safest harbour" along the southern coast of the Bristol Channel. Doubtless he was right: it was a busy trading port, not only with frequent traffic with South Wales and Ireland, but also eventually with the Mediterranean. Wool from Exmoor sheep was a major commodity, as indicated by a woolpack on the town's coat-of-arms.

The Lutterell family of nearby Dunster kept a fairy-godfatherly eye on the port's maintenance and improvement for centuries. About 250 years ago it even developed a sizeable ship-building industry. But the 19th-century saw many changes and by the start of the present century the town had become a resort and now Defoe's "best port" accommodates a few coastal fishing vessels and a huddle of private yachts and lesser pleasure craft. And at the eastern end of the town's coastline is that popular 20th-century phenomenon, a large holiday camp.

Yet much of the old-time Minehead remains in this, one of Somerset's oldest towns, whose name derives from the Celtic word "mynedd", a hill. Towering above the flat and frivolous coastal area is the very steep hill. On it has stood for half a millenium, amid some lovely houses and cottages, the church. It is appropriately dedicated to St. Michael, the saint traditionally associated with hills and peaks.

On one side, far below, is the sea. To landward, the great 1,564-foot eminence of Dunkery Beacon, the highest point and northern culmination of the great Forest of Exmoor.

MONTACUTE

Four miles from the busy industrial town of Yeovil is the quiet village of Montacute, so named from the neighbouring steep conical hill, described by the Normans as *mons acutus.* The Conqueror kept it in the family by granting it to his half-brother Robert, Count of Mortaigne, but Robert's castle has vanished and in its place is a "folly" tower erected in the 18th-century. In the village was a Cluniac priory. When Henry VIII dissolved it in 1539 he leased it to Sir William Petre. But it was the Phelips family who are indelibly associated with Montacute: they had settled there sixty years before the priory's dissolution.

A few yards from the attractive village inn, the Phelips Arms, is the entrance to the finest gem of late Elizabethan architecture in all Wessex: Montecute House.

Two years before Elizabeth I started her long reign, Thomas Phelips lived in a much more modest house (since demolished) but in 1588 he gave all his property to his youngest son, Edward – a shrewd move because Edward's three brothers were an unruly bunch and Edward was destined to become rich and influential, and to make possible the present superb Montacute House.

He was called to the Bar in 1579 and his energy and ability brought him a lucrative practice. He became a Member of Parliament in 1601, was appointed Serjeant-at-Law and King's Serjeant two years later, when he was knighted, and by 1604 he was Speaker of the House of Commons. It was Sir Edward Phelips who opened the prosecution for the Crown at the trial of Guy Fawkes. The summit of his career came in 1611, when he took up the highly lucrative job of Master of the Rolls.

MONTACUTE

The great Elizabethan house, built of local stone from Ham Hill, was completed by about 1601. Sir Edward Phelips employed a Somerset mason, William Arnold, as architect-craftsman for his fine new home. Arnold was later to gain great respect for his skill and honesty elsewhere, notably from Dorothy Wadham in the building of Wadham College, Oxford.

After Sir Edward's death in 1614, the Phelips family underwent a series of crises, financial, domestic and political. His successor, Sir Robert, a Member of Parliament, upset both Commons and King through his outspokenness on various issues. He was arrested at Montacute and spent eight months in the Tower of London.

In the Civil War Robert's son Edward and his brother, Robert, fought for the King. But when things looked really grim for the Royalist cause Edward, fearful of forfeiting his estate, pulled out and paid a fine imposed by Parliament. But Robert, having no estate to lose, did not defect: he fought at the battle of Worcester and helped Charles II to escape to France.

Complicated wills, family disputes and the shadow of insolvency bedevilled succeeding owners of Montacute. Relief came occasionally through astute marriages and, in the 18th-century, two very welcome inheritances actually justified improvements being made to the house.

But in the early part of the present century – the family silver and other valuables having already been sold – the estate was disposed of and the house was leased, in 1911, for an annual rental of £650.

The Parlour

MONTACUTE

In 1915 the Marquess Curzon of Kedleston became the tenant, paying only £550 a year. A former Viceroy of India, he was a man who in many respects belonged to a past century.

Montacute's noble tenant, in consideration of a reduced rental, agreed to re-decorate the house and instal electric light. For advice on *decor* he enlisted the services of Elinor Glyn, the "daring" novelist of the period, whose best-known work, *Three Weeks,* was avidly read – but secreted behind cushions when grandma came to tea. Elinor Glyn, an admirer of Curzon, stayed at Montacute to supervise the decorations. In Curzon's bedroom the visitor will see a framed photograph of her.

While at Montacute, Curzon was to face the most agonising suspense of his proud life. His three ambitions had been to be Captain of Oppidans at Eton, Viceroy of India and Prime Minister. There was then only the third to achieve. In 1923 Andrew Bonar Law resigned the Premiership and Curzon, who was Foreign Secretary, fully expected to succeed him. Although he had installed electricity, there was no telephone at Montacute but at last a telegram from the King's Private Secretary arrived, summoning him to London. But on arrival he learned the shattering news that the King had assented to the ministerial advice of the appointment of Stanley Baldwin.

The noble marquess, during the hours of waiting, had perhaps been unable to adjust to the fact that by the year 1923 it had long been unacceptable to have a Prime Minister without a seat in the Commons – even though he may be a Most Superior Person, as he was mockingly known since undergraduate days.

MONTACUTE

After Curzon's lease ended in 1929, circumstances compelled Mr. Gerard Phelips to sell. The house was valued at the derisory sum of £5,882 "for scrap", and lingered on the market for two years. Mercifully, rescue work was afoot: it was bought for the Society for the Protection of Ancient Buildings by Mr. Ernest Cook (the travel agent) and given to the National Trust. But, except for 23 family portraits and elegant 18th-century library armchairs which remain on loan from Mr. David Phelips, it was virtually bare of contents.

Then, in 1960, the Trust received specifically for the house a magnificent bequest of superb tapestries, furniture, paintings and ceramics from another benefactor, Sir Malcolm Stewart. Other splendid gifts and loans were also made.

Even more was to come. In 1975 the empty Long Gallery was restored by the Trust and the National Portrait Gallery, and on its walls now hang 16th and 17th century portraits from the Gallery's own collection. In the central recesses are portraits of Kings and Queens of England.

The National Portrait Gallery at Montacute House is available at the Trust's shop. The Trust's own scholarly, detailed and illustrated story of the house and garden is a model of its kind.

It explains that "some rooms are sparsely equipped for historic and practical reasons; concerts and other events are held regularly in the Hall". And the booklet ends on this piquant note: "Today, visitors will find Elizabeth and her Court in permanent residence at Montacute: Sir Edward Phelips' expectations for the house are fulfilled at long last".

Sir Edward Phelips

NETHER STOWEY

Pleasant rather than picturesque, the village – once a small market town – has an assured place in literary history through its association with Samuel Taylor Coleridge, the poet, philosopher and mystic, who lived and wrote there his greatest poem, *The Rime of the Ancient Mariner,* as well as *Kubla Khan* and part of *Christabel,* all in the space of three years from 1797. His home, once thatched, is occupied by a family but owned by the National Trust and a parlour containing fascinating Coleridge miscellanea is open to the public.

It was through a local man that Coleridge and his family came to Stowey: Thomas Poole, a self-educated and successful tanner with a taste for literature and languages (he taught himself French and Italian) and a village benefactor.

When William Wordsworth and his sister Dorothy came to live at Alfoxton Park, Holford, they were frequent visitors to Coleridge, walking the four miles along the edge of the Quantocks, past lovely Shervage Wood (now National Trust) to talk for hours, planning new forms of poetry.

But poets, be they mystic or idyllic, can plan other things as well as verse. With a war against Napoleon and simmering unrest in England, Coleridge and the Wordsworths and a coterie of other Radical intellectuals indulged at Stowey in some wild political discussions which brought them under suspicion locally to the extent that (as we have seen on the page about the Wordsworths at Alfoxton) the government sent an agent to enquire into the possible danger to the State.

Coleridge's Cottage

Cottage interior

NETHER STOWEY

Poets and Radicals apart, many imagine that Nether Stowey has nothing of historical interest to offer. Today, this is understandable because a bye-pass road has amputated an interesting and important limb – Stowey Court and church. Nevertheless, the new road is a blessing, since it has diverted the through traffic on the Bridgwater to Minehead road and left the village where Coleridge dwelt to mind its own affairs in reasonable tranquility.

Lord Audley started building the Court, but it was unfinished when his lordship was executed for supporting the rebellion of the Yorkist Pretender, Perkin Warbeck, who himself was hanged in 1499. Building was resumed in Elizabeth's reign and finished in 1588 – "Armada Year".

Except for the tower, the present church was rebuilt in the 19th-century and contains a memorial tablet to Tom Poole, Coleridge's Stowey friend and admirer. Among his other benefactions and social activities, Poole founded the Stowey Woman's Friendly Society in 1806. To this day it publicly marks its existence in a most charming way.

Starting from the clock tower in the hub of the village, opposite the Rose and Crown and the George inns, a host of women (and children, too) gathers on an appointed day in June. They carry bunches of flowers. Stowey's traditional "Women's Walk" then goes in procession to the church for a service, returning to the Rose and Crown for a festive tea.

Since the coming of the wide bye-pass, the walkers have to cross it – at a point opposite the charming 18th-century gazebo on the garden wall of the Court. But such modern perils do not deter the good womenfolk of Stowey.

NORTON ST. PHILIP

Once celebrated for its cloth fair, the village of Norton St. Philip is dominated by the splendid George inn which has an historic association through the Duke of Monmouth and a gossipy one through Samuel Pepys seventeen years before him. Architecturally, it is among the most interesting medieval inns in the kingdom. The ground floor is of stone but the overhanging upper structure is timbered. It has a staircase outside as well as within, and its galleried rear part is approached under an impressive archway. The stone part of the building may well indicate that it was originally a hostel for guests visiting the Carthusian priory at nearby Hinton Charterhouse.

In the summer of 1668 Pepys, with his Somerset-born wife and a small retinue left Frome after an overnight stop ("our beds good, but lousy; which made us merry") and called at the George at "Philip's Norton" for midday dinner, where the diarist records that they "dined very well, 10s". It was an extended dinner-hour, for Pepys took time to visit the church and inspect the tombstone of two sisters, the "Fair Maids of Fosscott", whose bodies had been joined "at the belly" since birth – Siamese Twins as they would be called today. The party then went on to Bath.

Shortly before meeting defeat at Sedgemoor in 1685 the Duke of Monmouth quartered his pathetic but enthusiastic followers in the neighbourhood, where there was a skirmish. The Duke made his headquarters at the George.

A prowling enemy of his cause spotted him at an upper window and took a pot shot at him with a musket. Had it not missed its mark, the Monmouth Rebellion would have ended at Norton St. Philip.

The George Inn

The Castle

NUNNEY

In the quiet and charming little village of Nunney, down a hill off the Frome-Shepton Mallet road, are the substantial remains of a moated castle. Village, castle and church together give Nunney a fairy-tale air unmatched by any other place in east Somerset.

The castle's appearance is more characteristic of a French fortified building than of a traditionally English one of its period. This may be explained by the fact that in 1372 Sir John de la Mere returned, rich with plunder, from the wars with France. Edward III gave him permission to fortify his house and castle; building began the following year.

The castle, now an empty but immensely impressive shell, became a victim of the Civil War. Colonel Richard Prater, a Royalist and a Roman Catholic, was then the manorial lord. The Parliamentary army, with Cromwell and Fairfax, had been successful in Dorset and was heading for Bristol via Castle Cary and Shepton Mallet in September, 1645. It was thought (erroneously, as it proved) that the castle contained a big store of ammunition. Two regiments were accordingly diverted from the main army with orders to capture the castle with the ammunition intact.

The Parliamentary force was equipped with artillery which they sited on rising ground facing the north wall of the castle. The garrison of about 80 was a mixed lot, and for the most part Irish mercenaries. It is highly likely that a deserter divulged the thinnest part of the walls, where a staircase led to the living quarters. Within two days the wall was breached and the castle's casualties were nil – except for one deserter.

Colonel Prater surrendered; but that was not the end of the story.

NUNNEY

Colonel Prater did more than surrender – he actually went so far as to offer to change sides! But his defection proved useless in securing the entity of his property. In accordance with its usual policy, Parliament later saw to it that the castle was rendered useless as a fortress and dwelling-place. Moreover, Prater's entire estate was confiscated by the Commonwealth.

After the Restoration, Colonel Prater's son George recovered the castle remains and the estate from the King, but later sold them. On Christmas Day, 1910, part of the wall which had been breached by Cromwell's artillery eventually collapsed. And in 1926 the then owner and lord of the manor, Mr. Robert Bailey-Neale, transferred the ruins to the guardianship of the Commissioners of H. M. Works (now the Department of the Environment); some necessary clearance and consolidation work was carried out and preservation was assured for posterity.

Those who wish to cross the 25-feet wide moat and enter the castle may now do so by taking a charmingly leisurely and informal course. In the main street of the village, opposite a picturesque stone bridge which spans a tributary of the river Frome, one knocks at a cottage door. Within, a cheerful lady issues admittance tickets and entrusts one with the key of the castle. At the padlocked gate by the moat one uses the key, making sure to re-lock the gate after entry. On re-crossing the moat after viewing the castle, the same procedure of unlocking and re-looking is observed before returning the key to the cottage.

How exquisitely tranquil is the pace of life in this lovely spot since 1645!

PORLOCK

Romantic legend precedes a thousand years of recorded history in lovely Porlock and its coastal neighbour Porlock Weir, on the Bristol Channel near Somerset's border with Devon.

Its church is dedicated to Dubricius, a Welsh Saint of early Britain, who died in the year 612. From the mists of antiquity comes the story that he crowned King Arthur at Caerleon and solemnised his marriage to Guinevere. Circumstantial evidence strongly suggests that the Saint's missionaries crossed the Bristol Channel to establish a church, and dedicated it to Dubricius.

In the ninth century came pagan Danish invaders to burn, loot and ravage, and early in the tenth the stout Porlockians repulsed a force from Britanny.

From the Norman Conquest the lordship of the manor belonged to several families, by descent or purchase, notably the Haringtons and eventually the Blathwayts, in whose hands it still remains. The history of the manors of those two families is told elsewhere, respectively under Kelston and Dyrham, both now in the county of Avon.

Under the thatches and tiles of Porlock today some 1,400 residents live in picturesque peace – including the noisiest, a Town Crier, complete with lace ruff and tricorn hat – but its visitors naturally number tens of thousands.

The Poet Laureate, Robert Southey (1774-1843), extolled its virtues in verse "written by an alehouse fire" at the cosy Ship Inn. A good touchstone of Porlocks charming transition from time past to the present day is Dovery Court, the fine 15th-century manor-house (on earlier foundations). It is now Porlock's Information Centre – with the added attraction of a billiards-room!

Porlock Weir

SEDGEMOOR

A few miles south of Edington, where King Alfred's defeat of the Danes led to the Treaty of Wedmore in the year 878, the last battle on English soil was fought on 6 July, 1685: the Battle of Sedgemoor, which in effect took little more than one hundred minutes to crush the claim of the Protestant Duke of Monmouth, the illegitimate son of Charles II and Lucy Walter, to the throne occupied by his uncle, James II.

Sedgemoor's flat terrain is intersected by watercourses known as rhines, often fringed with withies (willows), the raw material for basket-making. One of these, the Bussex Rhine, played a tactically vital part in the battle.

Monmouth, a talented solider with experience on European battlefields, was cornered in Bridgwater when the King's army of picked regulars under Lord Faversham, with John Churchill as second-in-command, were based at Westonzoyland. A villager from Chedzoy came to Bridgwater and offered to guide Monmouth across the Moor so that a surprise attack could be made in darkness. The Duke must have known that night attacks are extremely hazardous operations. His army of 3,500 men consisted mostly of untrained and ill-armed country folk. But the situation was critical, and he decided to go ahead.

His force marched in darkness silently out of Bridgwater, guided by the Chedzoy man, in a devious route to avoid Faversham's patrols. Monmouth had taken a desperate gamble and had a sporting chance of winning, but for a hitch in the plan which, before fighting took place, deprived him of his essential ally: the element of surprise.

The moor

SEDGEMOOR

The hitch which virtually lost the battle occured before it was joined, when Monmouth's men were crossing Langmoor Rhine on their way to Bussex Rhine, behind which were the sleeping troops of the royalists. The rebels' devious route had so far avoided the night patrols but at Langmoor they were discovered, only about 1,300 yards from their objective, by a patrol from Chedzoy. A shot was fired and it raised the alarm.

At a small road junction near Chedzoy a solitary signpost points laconically "To the Battle". Those who follow the route are advised first to obtain locally a graphic account of the entire operation in a booklet by John F. Lawrence, published by the Sedgemoor Preservation Society. When Monmouth saw that all was lost he fled before dawn but was captured in Hampshire and, within nine days of the fight, was beheaded in London.

With the coming of daylight the King's troops disgraced themselves, shooting the disarmed rebels for sport as they started them up, like game, from their hiding places on the Moor. Foremost in the savagery were the notorious "Kirke's Lambs". Colonel Percy Kirke had been Governor of Tangier, part of childless Katharine of Braganza's dowry when she became Queen on her marriage to Monmouth's father, Charles II.

History plays with words as well as with lives. Monmouth's bid for the throne was a "Rebellion' and unsuccessful rebels must expect death. But three years after Sedgemoor the invading force of William of Orange was marching through Somerset and his successful enterprise which gave him the throne became "The Glorious Revolution".

The battlefield

Westonzoyland Church

SEDGEMOOR

Westonzoyland's magnificent church, built mainly in the 15th-century by the penultimate Abbot of Glastonbury, became a prison after the battle. Its parish archives tell a piteous tale of the fight and its immediate aftermath. The contemporary chronicler tells us that the engagement began between one and two o'clock, a.m. and continued nearly an hour and a half. He continues: "there was killed upon the spott of the King's souldiers sixteen; five of them buried in the church, the rest in the churchyard, and they had all of them Christian buriall. There was killed of the Rebels upon the spott about 300, hanged with us 22 of which 4 were hanged in gemmasses (chains). About 500 prisoners brought into our church, of which there was 79 wounded and 5 of them died of their wounds in our church".

Perhaps those prisoners who survived incarceration at Westonzoyland were unlucky, for they had to await the fearful and infamous Bloody Assize of Judge Jeffreys, the creature of King James. Somerset and the westcountry in general paid heavily and the victims were mostly simple, Protestant country folk, and some gentry. The Assize was held at Taunton, Wells, Winchester, Salisbury, Dorchester and Exeter. At least 300 were hanged or otherwise executed and more than 800 were transported. Some few got away with a mere whipping.

It is little consolation to the victims of such unjustified vengeance that during the "Glorious Revolution" of 1688, George, first Baron Jeffreys was captured when trying to flee the country – and died a prisoner, in the Tower of London.

SHEPTON MALLET

This Mendip town, known in the vernacular as "Shep'n", derives the second part of its name from the ancient family of Mallet, whose escutcheon today bears no fewer than 28 quarterings. The manor first came into their possession in the 12th-century. Subsequent centuries saw the estate (twice confiscated by the Crown) in periods of other ownership. In 1536 the lordship was granted to the Prince of Wales, as Duke of Cornwall; and so it has remained.

An affray at the market place was the first taste of Civil War experienced in Somerset. A party of armed Royalists from Wells came to publish a document giving power to those named in it to raise troops for the King. Their coming had become known to Colonel William Strode of Downside, a Deputy Lieutenant, staunch Parliamentarian and a highly respected and wealthy Shepton clothier. The opposing parties' arrival in the town coincided; high words were exchanged, swords and pistols were drawn, Strode was unhorsed.

On the very same spot on a wet June day,another member of the Strode family, Edward, presented the impecunious Duke of Monmouth with one hundred guineas in support of his cause. The townsfolk gave the Duke a jubilant reception.

Today, history and contemporary life meet dramatically in the town. Its centre, which Monmouth knew, has been most intelligently re-developed, due largely to the influence of Francis Showering, a member of a Shepton family, manufacturers of sparkling perry, He financed the venture. From the nearby Showering factory the cheeky effigy of a baby chamois looks out upon a thriving and historic town.

Market Cross

SOMERTON

Somerset derives its name from the small and tranquil town of Somerton, deep in the low-lying heartland between Glastonbury and Ilminster. Ina, the warrior-king of Wessex (whose reign ended with abdication in 726) established supremacy over all England south of the Thames and under him Somerton enjoyed the status of a royal borough. The Saxon fort was succeeded by a medieval castle. The White Hart inn is believed to occupy part of the site.

The attractive market cross was rebuilt in Stuart times and forms the cynosure of the lovely little town.

Somerton can claim natives who made their mark in antiquarianism, divinity, art and topography.

The orientalist Joseph Sams (1784-1840) travelled afar collecting and cataloguing European and Eastern antiquities. Although failing to gain adequate recognition in his own lifetime Marmaduke Cradock (1660-1716), a house-painter's apprentice (wrongly called "Luke") was an artist specialising in pictures of animals and birds, also still-life. It was not until twenty-seven years after his death that engravings of his work were produced.

Richard Newcomb (d. 1769) was a celebrated topographical draughtsman whose *magnum opus* was a map of London and suburbs, published in 1658. Only two copies exist.

An immense stir was caused by the Somerton-born Nonconformist Divine, Humphrey Philips (1633-1707). A Fellow of Magdalen College, Oxford, he was sacked in 1660 and actually imprisoned in 1662. On release he went to Holland but later returned to his native land, where he was much persecuted. It was a rough time for outspoken Nonconformists!

Market Cross

STOGURSEY

Off the Quantock Hills, in a vale between Nether Stowey and the "Severn Sea", Stogursey lies quietly, almost unobtrusively, yet its history, seldom placid, is a very long one. Norman and some later relics remain, notably in the interior of its magnificent, and lovingly cared for, parish church.

William the Conqueror, born in the Normandy town of Falaise, bestowed it upon his fellow-townsman and namesake, William de Falaise. Then it passed into the possession of another Norman family, the de Courcys. Stogursey's name is a comparatively modern corruption of Stoke de Courcy. In the 12th-century John de Courcy, a doughty warrior and (so legend has it) a prodigious trencherman, left his Somerset castle to achieve the conquest of Ireland, becoming the first Earl of Ulster and Baron Kingsale – the oldest Irish barony. From the king he was granted the right to stand before the monarch with his head covered: a right still belonging to the holder of the barony.

Stogursey was held through the centuries by a diversity of noble, and often ferocious, families. Few places in Somerset can retain marks of so long a chain of historical eras. It even nudges this epoch-making atomic age, for at Hinkley Point on the nearby coast – not far from where John de Courcy set sail to conquer Ireland – is now an atomic power station.

Another aspect of modern times is reflected by the present John de Courcy, the 35th Baron Kingsale, born in 1941. Before and since serving in the Army (predictably with the Irish Guards) he lists in *Who's Who* his activities as including those of a film extra, a property developer, a white hunter – and a Bingo Caller!

The Parish Church

TARR STEPS

Most of the real heart of Exmoor Forest is desolate, treeless, boggy country. Its wild beauty has little to offer in terms of recorded history, but its vast and soggy uplands give birth to the headwaters of brooks and streams flowing north and south from its heights, later to become rivers – notably the West Lyn making its way to the Bristol Channel and the Exe taking its southerly course to the English Channel.

In the wild country north of the Simonsbath-Challacombe road (B3358) is the marshy ground of Exe Head and west of it, brooding in its desolation, is Pinkworthy ("Pinkery") Pond, the source of the Barle. The Pond was created long since by damming, but the work of its enterprising "developer" of a quagmire now stands forlorn: a ghostly spot.

The lovely little Barle is a real river by the time it reaches Withypool: it flows into the Exe at Dulverton, but some miles before that confluence it races under Tarr Steps, claimed to be the oldest bridge in England, in a setting of great natural beauty. The age of this clapper-bridge, 180 feet long, has never been determined, but it may well belong to pre-history.

In the summer of 1952 a period of continuous heavy rain saturated all Exmoor and culminated in an appalling deluge on 15 August. A 12-feet high flood even swept downstream the vast stones of Tarr Steps. The flood disaster not only affected the Barle and Exe valleys, but to the north the raging river Lyn destroyed many houses in Devon's Lynmouth, with considerable loss of life.

Each one of the stones of Tarr Steps has since been fully restored to its original place.

TAUNTON

Here is Somerset's heart. On the river Tone, with the "green hills of Somerset" bordering the fertile and lovely Vale of Taunton Deane, the busy town of Taunton has an ancient, and sometimes tragic, history.

King Ina, extending the West Saxon kingdom into western Somerset, fortified it in the 8th-century; it was a mint town at the time of the Norman Conquest; the imposter Perkin Warbeck captured it in the reign of Henry VII; the Civil War found it between the upper and nether millstones of King and Parliament. It was held by the Roundheads in 1642, by the Royalists in the following year and in 1645 by the Somerset-born Parliamentarian, Robert Blake, who withstood a long siege. At the Restoration of Charles II it was punished by having its defensive walls demolished.

Taunton's history reached its most memorable and subsequently tragic stage in the summer of 1685 when James Scott, Duke of Monmouth, was proclaimed king at the Market Cross. The Protestant Duke, claimant to the throne occupied by his uncle, James II, was a handsome and romantic figure, welcomed throughout the west by the country folk and town tradesmen, though many of the landed gentry prudently remained aloof: they had more to lose if things went wrong.

Monmouth's recruiting journey from Lyme through Somerset was an emotional one. At Taunton, in the course of the general acclamation, emotion reached its zenith.

A bevy of maidens from a local seminary for young ladies publicly presented the glamorous Duke with a Bible, also a banner which they had embroidered for him.

The old castle

The castle entrance

TAUNTON

Soon after leaving Taunton the Duke was defeated at Sedgemoor and the Monmouth Rebellion was over. A few weeks later Taunton was the scene of one of the most atrocious sessions of the Bloody Assize, presided over by the infamous Lord Chief Justice Jeffreys.

It was held in the Great Hall of the Castle and sat for only two days, but in that period no fewer than 509 rebels faced the grisly charade of a "trial", for although there was a jury, the jurors were bullied, browbeaten and usually ignored by the unspeakable Jeffreys. All but one of the prisoners were sentenced to death and hanged in public places throughout the area.

Within three years Jeffreys himself was dead, when a prisoner in the Tower of London, but his likeness remains in the Great Hall at Taunton Castle: a portrait of him looks down on what is now an utterly different scene, for the Castle now houses the splendid Somerset County Museum.

There is another echo of the Monmouth Rebellion near the Castle, a small area called Tangier. It refers to the place where Colonel Percy Kirke's Tangier Regiment ("Kirke's Lambs") was billeted in 1685. As described under the heading of "Sedgemoor", the "Lambs" were notorious for their cruelty to the defeated rebels after the battle.

Unsuccessful rebels may expect to pay a high price for failure, but Jeffreys and Kirke made a loathsome pair, prostituting alike the law and the profession of arms.

Tudor House

TAUNTON

Judge Jeffreys' victims were not entirely confined to simple Protestant rustics and townsfolk who died for their beliefs. One of the gentlemen who paid the penalty was Captain Abraham Annesley, who expressed in poignant words the feeling which must have been so deep and sincere throughout the west country. Speaking from the scaffold at Taunton he declared: "... *for had I a thousand lives they should all be engaged in the same cause*".

"The Tudor House" in Fore Street, a fine example of half-timbered domestic architecture bearing the date 1578, was the home of Taunton's Member of Parliament, Sir William Portman. When Monmouth was proclaimed king, Sir William was in London attending Parliament but by the time of the battle of Sedgemoor he was back in his constituency and during the Bloody Assize Judge Jeffreys was his house-guest. Portman's house (scheduled as an Ancient Monument) is now a restaurant and the room he made available for Jeffreys can be seen by the public.

But before the Bloody Assize, which followed so swiftly after Sedgemoor in that summer of 1685, Portman had played a vital part for King James.

Immediately after Monmouth had fled from the lost battle, armed parties scoured the countryside in search of the hapless Duke. Sir William happened to be in the group which captured him.

Doubtless because of his status, it was Portman who was in charge of the guard which took the prisoner to London – and to death by the headsman's axe.

TAUNTON

Taunton's history is so dominated in the public mind by the Monmouth episode that it is well to be reminded of its less lurid story both before and since 1685: its seats of learning, its almshouses, its architecture. The town has a happy genius for blending and adapting the past with the present.

A grammar school existed at Taunton in 1273 and in 1522 Bishop Foxe (bishop of Winchester and founder of Corpus Christi College, Oxford) built and endowed his school there. The present building, providing a pleasant contrast to the fortified castle nearby, is now the seat of the Taunton Deane District Council. But the 19th-century saw the foundation at Taunton of a trio of notable schools, all now Public Schools: Queen's College in 1843, Taunton School in 1847 and King's College (so named to commemorate the Wessex king, Alfred the Great) in 1869.

Of architectural interest are Gray's and Huish's almshouses, both founded in the early 17th-century, and an architectural cynosure is St. Margaret's Hospital – a long, whitewashed building with thatched roof. It was founded in 1160 as a leper hospital and later became an institution for the poor, but is now used by the Somerset Rural Community Council and the Somerset Guild of Craftsmen.

In the late Georgian period the town benefited from the wealth and good taste of one of its sons, Sir Benjamin Hammet – banker, property developer and M.P. for his native town. The houses on either side of elegant Hammet Street, brick-built and with porticos, were erected in 1778. At the end of the street stands in happy contrast the magnificent tower of the church of St. Mary Magdalene, surely among the grandest of the pinnacled towers so characteristic of Somerset Churches.

St Margaret's Hospital

THORNBURY

Dark and dirty deeds, deceit and double-dealing, vindictiveness and vanity marked the early history of Thornbury, a trim little town near the Severn north of Bristol.

The manor was inherited in 1020 by Berthric, a Saxon (sometimes known as Brihtric) who became England's ambassador to the court of the powerful Baldwin, Count of Flanders. His daughter Matilda, a beautiful and talented woman, fell in love with the envoy and, as was customary for females of more exalted rank than their intended husbands, she proposed marriage to him. But Berthric turned her down – and hastened back to England.

Then, Duke William of Normandy wooed Matilda. As he was a bastard, the lady infuriated him by hinting that his illegitimacy was one of the reasons for her refusal. But William would not take "no" for an answer. Once he waylaid and beat her to the ground as she returned from Mass; later he boldly stalked in to her father's castle and, in her mother's presence, dragged her off literally by her hair. Matilda presumably admired the cave-man treatment and they married.

After William conquered England in 1066, his wife played a vindictive trick on her old love, Berthric. She not only persuaded her husband to dispossess him and give his Thornbury manorial lands to her, but also had the poor fellow thrown into prison at Winchester, where he died in 1068.

Matilda's manor passed from royal hands on the accession of her eldest son, William Rufus, and its history was later dominated by the family of Humphrey Stafford, created first Duke of Buckingham in 1444. Henry, the second Duke, was beheaded in 1483 for rising against Richard III, whom he had helped to acquire the throne!

THORNBURY

When the Tudor dynasty started in the person of Henry VII, that king restored to Edward, the third Duke of Buckingham, all the titles and estates of his executed father.

After the accession of Henry VIII (1509-1547) Buckingham became the most influential nobleman in the kingdom, holding the highest offices under the Crown, including Grand Master of the Horse, a post which in wartime ranked second only to the king himself and gave its holder command in the field in the absence of the monarch.

But the man who stood so high in royal favour and trust was to fall, as his father had done. A whispering campaign, started by a steward who had been sacked, reached the king (through Cardinal Wolsey) to the effect that Buckingham may pursue a claim to the throne on Henry's death. Although the story must have been based upon the very remote dynastic fact that Buckingham was a great-grandson of the youngest son of Edward III, the King being sensitive about the Tudor succession, decided to take pre-emptive action.

When Buckingham was at Thornbury, watching his castle a-building, he was arrested, taken to London, convicted of high treason and executed. The castle then became a royal residence. Henry paid it a brief visit with Anne Boleyn in 1533 and his daughter Mary lived there for several years under the guardianship of the bishop of Exeter. When she became Queen she made reparation to the Staffords, granting castle, manor and town to Lord Stafford, son of the hapless duke. The castle now is a restaurant of the first order. And a few yards from the gatehouse rises the noble tower of the parish church, its delicate pinnacles overlooking the unfinished castle, the sloping pasture-land and the Severn estuary beyond.

WATCHET

The tiny town and port of Watchet is almost as old as the hills behind it and the sea in front. Tribes of pre-history assembled there. In Saxon and Norman times it had a mint – but numismatists wishing to see original coins minted there will have to journey to the County Museum at Taunton; to the British Museum in London; or to the Royal Cabinet Collection in Stockholm!

That immaculate dresser Charles I is said to have worn a waistcoat of "Watchet blue". The reason for this special colour is obscure. Some say it derives from woad, that blue cosmetic which our distant ancestors treated their skin so liberally; others aver that the name had its birth from the coloured albaster found in nearby cliffs.

Watchet throve apace during the Industrial Revolution exporting iron ore from the Brendon Hills to the growing heavy industries in South Wales, just across the Bristol Channel, and importing coal. Prosperity declined sadly towards the end of the 19th-century, capped by the destruction of its harbour and the ships lying there in 1900. A terrific gale coincided with exceptionally high tides, whose ebb and flow in the Channel is one of the highest in the world.

Undaunted, the townsfolk raised the money and a stone harbour was built. From its pier-end one can see on the skyline the lofty peak which overlooks Minehead; and tucked away from visitors' sight a modern paper mill and other industrial activity has re-born picturesque Watchet, now a thriving community boasting annual exports exceeding £25 million. Yet the historic past blands with the present. The ancient Court Leet still exists and a Portreeve is elected annually.

The Quay

WEDMORE

While Athelney is of all places in Somerset the most popularly known in connection with Alfred the Great because of the timeless story of the burnt cakes, after his defeat of the Danes in the area the most significant place was Wedmore, for it was there that the victorious king concluded peace with them in the year 878. In 1978, spaced throughout May, June and July the village nobly marked the eleven hundredth anniversary of the Treaty of Wedmore in a series of sparkling celebrations: a mock battle and a Saxon feast; a fair; a pageant, flower festival and music programmes.

In the ancient parish church, which dominates serenly the charming village, the thousandth anniversary of Alfred's death – in 901 – is commemorated on a tablet.

Wedmore's keen sense of history and royal anniversaries is evidenced elsewhere in the church. The great west window, known as the "history window", is of modern stained glass and depicts a galaxy of historic personages and occasions.

The window commemorates Queen Victoria's Jubilee. At the top are depicted the heads of three sovereigns who also attained Jubilees: Henry III (1216-1272), Edward III (1327-1377) and George III (1760-1820).

Below, in full-length, are seen two kings and two queens regnant: Alfred the Great, William the Conqueror, Elizabeth I and Victoria.

Notable events in the periods of those four monarchs are shown at the base of this remarkable window. They include Victoria's coronation, Harold's death at the Battle of Hastings, Elizabeth and the Spanish Armada, and Alfred – burning those memorable cakes at nearby Athelney!

WEDMORE

The historic past of the "Isle of Wedmore" is not confined to Alfred the Great. Eight centuries after his time a remarkable country doctor, whose family had been small landowners there since 1509, made his mark as a pioneer in the treatment of mental illness.

Dr. John Westover (1643-1706) was the son of a local doctor. He lived at Porch House and opened what was probably the first private residential lunatic asylum in the kingdom at "Westover's Barn", a few yards from his home. Both buildings are still standing and occupied as private dwellings.

Westover was a precise keeper of accounts and those parts of his journal which still exist reveal him to be also a conscientious and compassionate general practitioner, making what are now bureaucratically called "domiciliary visits" to cottagers and gentry alike and charging them, in cash or kind, strictly according to their means.

Some of his mentally sick patients appear to have been cured, though nothing is known of the good doctor's methods of treatment. Cases came from as far away as Gloucester, Bristol, Tiverton and Exeter. A year's board cost about £12, but patients could obtain "comforts" such as playing cards, hair powder and tobacco.

It is significant that some pages of Dr. Westover's journal, written soon after Monmouth's defeat at Sedgemoor, have been torn out. Almost certainly this was to destroy evidence that the compassionate doctor, true to the Hippocratic Oath, had given succour to some fugitives. Even so, at Wedmore the price for unsuccessful rebellion was seen to have been paid: two rebels were hanged there.

The field still bears the name "Hangacre".

Porch House and Westover's Barn

The obelisk

WELLINGTON

A soldier made famous the name of this delectable little town astride the highway from Taunton to Exeter. It gave the titles of viscount, earl and duke to the Irish family of Wellesley, although Arthur Wellesley, victor of Waterloo and first Duke of Wellington, is believed to have visited the place only once – five years after taking his ducal title from it.

Nevertheless, the townsfolk commemorated the Iron Duke in fine style. On the steep escarpment of the Blackdown Hills south of their town they erected an obelisk which dominates the countryside and offers superb views across to the Quantock Hills and Exmoor.

The town pre-dates Alfred the Great, who owned the manor and bestowed it upon the see of Wells. On its southern outskirts is the admirable Wellington School (the Public School for boys, not to be confused with the perhaps more widely known Wellington College in Berkshire) founded in the 19th-century, when the town could claim as natives or residents some distinguished writers and editors in the fields of anthropology, lexicography and divinity. In the heart of the town was born Thomas Spencer Baynes, the encyclopaedist and journalist, who became editor of *Encyclopaedia Britannica,* now an American-owned publication. A man with a universal mind, he was a master of the written word, his finest journalism appearing in the London *Daily News,* of which he was appointed assistant editor in 1858.

Baynes's article on the death of the Prince Consort in 1861 elicited private enquiries as to its authorship from Queen Victoria, who sent him a special message of thanks.

WELLS

Standing in the southern lee of the Mendips and facing the flat marshlands of central Somerset, Wells is a gem: small, compact and of immense historic and architectural interest. It is the smallest city in England and since the topographical surgery which created the new county of Avon in 1974, it is the only city in Somerset. Its name is derived from the springs near the Cathedral and open channels of water still run alongside the busy market-place, and beyond.

Its story begins with the foundation of a church near the source of the water supply by a Saxon king. Since 909 it has been the seat of a see, except for an interregnum when the Normans moved it to Bath in 1080 – and in so doing started a wrangle which was not resolved until a century later, when the monks of Bath elected Jocelyn as bishop; he re-established the see at Wells, his birthplace. The *coup* vastly annoyed Bath, but a neat compromise was reached by Jocelyn's successor, Roger, that he designate himself as bishop of Bath *and* Wells. Thus Bath retained precedence in the title, but the cathedral and the episcopel palace – each now a glory of its kind – is at Wells.

From the market place, the cathedral may be approached through Penniless Porch, where beggars sought alms from those entering the precinct; and the palace through a separate and more impressive archway a few yards away, known as the Bishop's Eye – thence across a green and over a bridge spanning the palace moat.

The cathedral church and the bishop's palace form a close neighbourliness perhaps unique in England: a place where work and worship go hand-in-hand.

WELLS

The city's earliest charter came, predictably, from episcopal hands. In the 12th-century bishop Roger conferred it and established Wells as a borough. Its first royal charter was bestowed by King John in 1201, about the time when building began on the present cathedral. The latest charter, conferring city status, was granted in 1974 by Queen Elizabeth II.

Down the centuries bishops of Wells, and later of Bath and Wells, provide an analgam of saintliness and of ambition; of pious generosity and of avarice; of compassion and of ruthlessness. Yet the Cathedral, though comparatively small, is certainly one of the loveliest in the land and had been made so by the generosity of a succession of bishops!

Its most spectacular feature is undoubtedly the vast and ornate twin-towered west front, laden with tiers of canopied statues and dwarfing the entrance doors so that they seem like arched mouse-holes: a theatrical effect, in striking contrast to the tranquil dignity of the nave within.

Time has taken its toll on the elaborately embellished example of architectural exuberance, however, and in 1977 a nationwide appeal for £1,000,000 was launched, to undertake the lengthy and costly work of restoration.

The Queen, the Queen Mother and the Prince of Wales have made gifts to the appeal. It is the first completely Gothic Cathedral in Europe and 1978 marked the 800th anniversary of its foundation.

WELLS

Surrounded by a moat and with the remains of ramparts, the palace and grounds are open to the public (except the bishop's own living quarters) at certain times. Parties belonging to charitable and other organisations may sometimes be seen having a picnic on the lawn and the vaulted undercroft is fitted out as a refreshment room and can be "borrowed" for a variety of occasions. It is all in keeping with the spirit of Wells, which remains small enough to be neighbourly.

On an upper floor is the Long Gallery where hang portraits revealing much of the city's episcopal history. Among the earliest of some thirty portraits is that of the versatile Thomas Godwin. He was a headmaster in 1549 and a medical practitioner six years later; then he held the deaneries of Christ Church, Oxford, and of Canterbury before becoming bishop in 1584. He offended his Virgin Queen Elizabeth when he made a second marriage. Richard Fox, bishop from 1492-94 was the man who baptised Elizabeth's much-married father. He was more a soldier and diplomat than a priest and "arranged" the marriage of Henry VIII and Katharine of Arragon.

William Laud, who was to become archbishop of Canterbury and was beheaded in 1645, held the see briefly; and the high-handed William Pierse, bishop in 1632, was deprived of the see and sent to the Tower, though restored in 1660.

The episcopal galaxy also includes one bishop who temporarily exchanged his clerical garb for that of a cavalry commander: Peter Mews, whose portrait shows him sporting a large black patch on his left cheek. He fought against Monmouth at the battle of Sedgemoor in 1685 – and his face came into collision with a musket-ball.

Bishop's Palace

WELLS

Perhaps the most widely known of the bishops depicted in the Long Gallery is the beloved and courageous Thomas Ken, one of the "Seven Bishops" who petitioned against the Declaration of Indulgence, was deprived of his bishopric and spent his last days just outside Somerset's borders at Longleat as a guest of Lord Weymouth; but at his request his body was interred within his old see, at Frome. Ken's lasting memorial rests on his authorship of the doxology "Praise God from Whom all blessings flow" and for his hymns "Awake my soul and with the sun" and "Glory to Thee, my God, this night".

The portraits in the main gallery and adjoining rooms take us into present times: notably the intellectual William Wand, later Bishop of London, who died in 1977, and the genial William Bradfield, Wand's successor at Wells, who was bishop from 1946-1960.

"From time immemorial and since the memory of man runneth not to the contrary", at Coronations two specific bishops have been "supporters" on either side of the Monarch: Bath and Wells on the left side and Durham on the right. "Time immemorial" in this case dates from the crowning of Richard I in 1189 and the bishops' successors have retained the privilege ever since.

Terence Cuneo's splendid portrayal of the Coronation scene in 1953 is shown in the gallery, with William Bradfield's features distinctly limned. And in a case is displayed his Coronation Cope.

The Palace is on a site which has belonged to the Church for more than one thousand years.

Madonna and child

WELLS

In the area known as the Liberty – where once its dwellers were immune from arrest – is the Cathedral School, Somerset's oldest educational foundation. It occupies several interesting buildings.

Vicars Close, built about 1360, is claimed to be the oldest complete inhabited street in Europe. Facing Cathedral Green is an elegant house, formerly canonical, now the city museum. Here is told the local story from the Iron Age to the recent past, for it includes a push-or-pull wheelchair, with windscreen and hood – a "convertable" in modern motoring terms; and a few yards away are reminders of the Romans' mining activities in the Mendips: "piggs" of lead impressed with the name of Vespasian, who was elected Roman Emperor in AD 69.

The inns, now graced with the name hotel, are attractively enticing, as well as historic elements of the townscape, among them the Crown, the Red Lion, the Star and the Swan. In the 15th-century Bishop's Barn, now corporation-owned, one may play Badminton or attend an occasional auction sale. No less remarkable is the City Arms, a pub and steakhouse with a charming courtyard: for some three centuries it fulfilled a far less attractive function as the city's prison.

A long plaque set flush into the pavement in the Market Place is a very modern touch. It records that Mary Bignal Rand, born and reared in Wells, won an Olympic gold medal at Tokyo in 1964 with her long jump of 22 feet and 2¼ inches. The precise length is delineated on the pavement. The identify of the donor is modestly indicated by the initials TWW; but the citizens know that it was the gift of Television Wales and The West.

Vicar's close

WELLS

In the short and turbulent reign of Henry IV, Nicholas Bubwith was Treasurer of England. He became successively bishop of London, Salisbury and of Bath and Wells, dying at Wells in 1424. Bubwith bequeathed money to found and endow an almshouse in Chamberlain Street – then called Beggar Street – with the administration of which both Dean and Chapter and the City Corporation were initially concerned, and remain so to this day, under trustees appointed jointly.

The rooms accommodate a dozen residents and are flanked at the east end by a chapel (open to the public) and at the west by a large room built as a Guildhall and used as such until 1779, when the present Town Hall, off the Market Place, was erected. Bubwith's old Guildhall has been put to a more recreational use: it is now the residents' television lounge!

Since the good bishop's time, the range of buildings has attracted other benefactors, recorded there for all to see. In the 18th-century a city shopkeeper provided £50 and his sister later matched it with a similar sum. "An esquire" gave £306, and in 1774 the clergy weighed in, for we read that "the Bishop, his son the Chancellor and the Archdeacon 'confirmed' £1,200 in 3 per cent South Sea annuities or £36 per annum for ever". On his death in the early 19th-century Clement Tudway, who had been the M.P. for 55 years, gave £500 "and 3 per cent South Sea annuities and interest for ever £50 per annum".

In 1964 the foundation received £500 through Alderman Lilian M. Osmond's Mayoral appeal.

Bubwith's Almshouse

WELLS

Standing in splendour at the western end of the city is St. Cuthbert's, the largest parish church in Somerset.

Its magnificent pinnacled tower, 122 feet high and built in 1430, is matched by few in a county celebrated for its church towers and to those travelling towards the city the distant view of it is often initially mistaken for that of the cathedral's. The site has been a place of worship from earliest times and its dedication to Cuthbert, a Saxon, is thought to be due to a dream in which Alfred the Great saw that saint on the eve of his decisive victory over the Danes which culminated with the Treaty of Wedmore, a village a few miles from Wells.

Unlike the cathedral, which serves as a spiritual centre for the entire diocese, St. Cuthbert's has always been essentially a church for the citizens. The life of the laity centred around it and trade guilds were associated with its many altars. The Mayor and Corporation played a major part in its management.

Though substantially belonging to the Perpendicular period, the church's treasury, is part of the older, 13th-century church. It has seen an intriguing variety of uses since its function as a strong-room for church plate and other treasures. In the post-Reformation period, during the reign of Elizabeth I, it was used as an armoury. In 1685, after the battle of Sedgemoor some of the pathetic prisoners who had fought for Monmouth were incarcerated there for a while.

Chapter House Steps

WEST QUANTOXHEAD ('ST. AUDRIES')

This village, more popularly known as St. Audries, was the seat of Sir Alexander Acland-Hood – the first Lord St. Audries – rebuilt on the site of a feudal manor in the 19th-century. In 1934 it became St. Audries School, a public school for girls – set in a lovely timbered combe leading to the sea from the Quantock Hills: it is held in Trust for the Church of England by the National Society. The house and village church, near neighbours, were rebuilt in 1856 by Sir Peregrine Acland. On the coast, just beyond, where a stream cascades over a cliff to the sea, fossilised fragments of pre-history may be discovered at low tide. Mammoth tusks found there are displayed in the County Museum at Taunton.

The church is dedicated to St. Etheldreda, the 7th-century Abbess of far-off Ely.

A moving example of the craftsmanship and dedication of simple Somerset folk and pride in their small rural environment is found in some of the embellishments of this otherwise unremarkable 19th-century church. Angels on the roof corbals are carved from Quantock oak; the iron flower-stands were wrought by a villager; and a blacksmith from the nearby hamlet of Staple fashioned the wrought-iron chandelier and door ironwork. The good smith's grave, close to that of Lord St. Audries, is redolent of the spirit of Gray's *Elegy Written in a Country Churchyard,* for it bears this touching epitaph:

Francis Stone 1886-1965 Spent his life in this village. Blacksmith, Bell-ringer and Friend of all.

Woodspring Priory

WESTON-SUPER-MARE

This curiously named seaside town, where the Severn estuary debouches into the Bristol Channel, is a modern and immensely popular holiday resort. It achieved its distinguishing Latin suffix, indicating "by the sea", as long ago as 1348. In course of time the pronunciation of the word Mare became anglicised, to rhyme not with Mary but with a female horse.

Weston-super-Mare is in a District of the county of Avon named Woodspring, after a small but historic spot to the north of the town: Woodspring (originally Worspring) Priory.

It was founded early in the 13th-century by William de Courtenay, a descendant of Reginald Fitzurse, one of the murderers of Archbishop Thomas Becket in Canterbury Cathedral in 1170. At that time Woodspring was apparently one of the estates of Fitzurse, whose daughter Matilda married a de Courtenay.

The foundation at Woodspring was an act of expiation for his forbear's deed. Similarly in West Somerset, at Williton (as will be seen under that heading) Robert Fitzurse, brother of the assassin, had earlier founded a chapelry.

Standing serenely in a low-lying rural environment, yet so near the lively town of Weston-super-Mare, Woodspring has in the present century been threatened with, and escaped from virtual oblivion. "Bungaloid development" was envisaged, as was a scheme to convert the monastic church into an hotel, but happily neither materialised. The coastline and estate were acquired by the National Trust in 1968.

The Priory itself subsequently passed into the care of the Landmark Trust. After considerable restoration it was made available to the public in 1972.

WILLITON

Richard Fitzurse held the land at Williton and two years after his death in 1168 one of his sons, Reginald, joined three other knights in rushing off to Canterbury Cathedral: there they murdered the archbishop, Thomas Becket. Reginald is believed to have died in Jerusalem, while doing penance.

Another Fitzurse son, Robert, built a chapelry (perhaps in expiation of his brother's deed) which subsequently formed the foundation of Williton's parish church of St. Peter. After the Fitzurses there came in turn the families of Demborough, Sydenham, Orchard and Wyndham. The manor-house is called Orchard Wyndham and its oldest part is 15th-century. The house is still in Wyndham occupation.

Williton stands, immaculately attractive, at the radial point of four roads – to Bridgwater, Minehead, Taunton and to the little port of Watchet, whence Coleridge's fictitious "Ancient Mariner" set sail. The spruce little town has the virtue of combining charm with practicality: thatched houses, a large red sandstone bank; and architecturally imposing Poor Law workhouse now transformed into a hospital; its own newspaper, the *West Somerset Free Press,* which has impartially served the area since 1860, and a spacious old posting inn, the Egremont Hotel.

The Egremont's projecting sign painted in a style fairly reminiscent of that of Sir Thomas Lawrence, depicts the head of a balding man and his torso in a colourful military tunic.

The subject is the Earl of Egremont, a member of the Wyndham family. The earldom, created in 1750, became extinct in 1845. Nevertheless there is once again a Lord Egremont, the title having been revived by the creation of a barony in 1963 for the late John Wyndham of historic Petworth House, Sussex, who married Pamela Wyndham-Quin.

Old workhouse

WOOKEY HOLE

Mendip has many caves – some hundreds of "holes" as they are known – of which the series at Cheddar attract the most publicity, but at Wookey Hole, a couple of miles from Wells, are not only caves but also some unique and anachronistic bedfellows – paper-making by hand, and wax effigies.

First, the caves. It is customary, in Britain and abroad, for formations in prehistoric grottoes to be given high-flown descriptive names as part of the guides' spiel for the wide-eyed tourist. The object which up-stages all else at Wookey is the Witch.

Although the lady is a stalagmite, at least she has a respectable history in *recorded* legend. The celebrated chronicler and traveller, William of Worcester, mentioned her haggish contours and by 1694 she was named as the Witch. In the 18th-century a reverend gentleman visiting the caves recorded (without comment) what his guide had said: "the cavern had never had but one inmate, an old witch who had been turned years ago into stone, by a parson, as she was cooking a child which she had stolen from the village". The guide added that he had heard his grandmother say that her father remembered the wicked old woman.

Early in the present century Herbert Balch, the Mendip archaeologist and geologist, added a fact – and a query – to the Witch's story. His investigations revealed a hammered-out socket under the old girl's left breast and below it the remains of a wooden stake.

"Was some wretch", he asked, "a sacrifice to the guardian deity of the underworld, which this crude human form was supposed to represent?"

Paper drying loft

WOOKEY HOLE

The clear waters of the river Axe emerge from their cavernous Mendip birthplace at Wookey Hole, where before 1610 they were earning their living in the manufacture of paper by hand. In 1783 a watermark was registered for the mill's high-quality products.

Steam power was installed by the middle of the 19th-century. A London wholesale stationer, William Samuel Hodgkinson, became the proprietor – an ownership which was to remain in the family for more than one hundred years. By the time of his death in 1876, ten vats were producing the highest quality hand-made paper for banknotes, for drawing, for legal documents; also for writing paper, for which the indefaticable diarist and authoress, Queen Victoria, was a customer.

Almost all of the working mill as seen today was built by Hodgkinson and his sons.

It is not surprising that the boom led to an increase in the local population of workpeople. In the best tradition of 19th-century rural industrial paternalism (based on enlightened self-interest) the proprietor built dwellings, a school and a church, and catered for the recreational side of the life of his workforce by providing the instruments for the mill's brass band.

A visitor entering the mill today experiences graphic echoes of 19th-century rural industrial history. On the walls of the Rag House are detailed instructions, written in 1896 by the retiring manager for the guidance of his son and successor. In the Drying Loft is a "Card of Freedom" for the papermakers' union.

It bears the motto "United to Support but not Combined to Injure".

WOOKEY HOLE

Hodgkinson started his stationery business in London in 1715 – a forty-five years before the birth of the famous Swiss wax-modeller Marie Grosholtz, better known under her married name of Madame Tussaud. She died in 1850, the year that the Hodgkinsons arrived to make paper at Wookey Hole.

The date has an historical fascination because, in a sense, Marie Tussaud has, like the Hodgkinsons, gravitated to Wookey Hole. In 1973 the entire complex of caves, paper mills and other features was bought from the widow of the last Hodgkinson by "Madame Tussaud's", the renowed wax-works exhibition in London, whence Marie Tussaud had transferred it from France in 1802.

The purchase was not merely an investment in a tourist attraction. Madame Tussaud's use some old paper-drying lofts as a working studio-storeroom, to relieve their cramped and vulnerable storage accommodation in the cellars of their exhibition building in Baker Street, London.

Thus a few yards from the relics of cave-man, rhinocerous, hyaena and mammoth (not to mention the Witch), one sees shelf after shelf of wax effigies of the heads of the famous, stored for reference, also a "library" of moulds.

The mill temporarily ceased paper-making in 1972, but since Madame Tussaud's acquired the property in the following year the mill buildings have been restored and from 1976 handmade paper production has been resumed.

It is an activity straddling the river Axe which has an almost unbroken ancestry of well-nigh four centuries.